Praise for *Questioning Psychology: beyond theory and control*

Wherever in the world psychological helping is practised as a profession, this book spells wonderful trouble. A pebble in the pond or spanner in the works, it asks very important questions that are mainly bypassed or forgotten elsewhere. It is a joy to read. Brian Levitt writes accessibly, beautifully, with wisdom and in the best possible way, *personally*. The profession of counselling and psychotherapy desperately needs this book. It should be required reading for all students and practitioners. It is the book I have always wanted to write. Thankfully, Brian Levitt has written it better than I ever could, and I am better for having read it. There are lessons for us all here.

Pete Sanders, author, retired counsellor, trainer and clinical supervisor

This is a book for all those who want to learn more about what it means to truly help another person. There is much wisdom in it. It says many of the things that many of us think but don't say in light of the dominant narratives in psychology. It presents an empathic but important critique of the aspects of psychology that get in the way of persons truly connecting with and responding and listening to other people. These include scientific research, theories, diagnostic categories, words and people's preconceptions. While valuing the contributions of science, Levitt critically examines its limitations, as well as the limitations of any belief system that is held to too rigidly and blinds us to the reality of a genuine meeting with other people. This book articulates the soul of the helping relationship: authentic empathy, openness, and the prizing of the uniqueness of each individual.

Arthur C Bohart, Professor Emeritus, California State University, Dominguez Hills

QUESTIONING PSYCHOLOGY
BEYOND THEORY AND CONTROL

BRIAN E LEVITT

 PCCS BOOKS

First published 2019

PCCS Books Ltd
Wyastone Business Park
Wyastone Leys
Monmouth
NP25 3SR
UK

Tel +44 (0)1600 891509
contact@pccs-books.co.uk
www.pccs-books.co.uk

Questioning Psychology: beyond theory and control

British Library Cataloguing in Publication Data.
A catalogue record for this book is available from the British Library

ISBN 978 1 910919 48 4

Cover design by Jason Anscomb
Printed in the UK by TJ International, Padstow

Contents

For my husband, Noel,
my love always.
You are life's most beautiful gift to me.

delicate star stuff
we face each other
your magic
hidden by my fears

Acknowledgements

My first two books were edited volumes that brought together, through an overarching concept, people I admire, and I did my best to support their unique voices, while contributing chapters of my own. The book you are holding now is a departure for me, since the writing is entirely mine. That has been a unique experience of highs and lows, including the distinct non-joy of extended periods of writer's block and self-doubt: I don't have anything to say; it has all been said already; what I'm saying is boring and clumsy; no one will want to read this. On and on. Through it all, as it has been for so many years, my husband, Noel, was there, listening to me like no one else can, understanding me, comforting me, and helping me to find my way back and to find clarity where it didn't seem possible. He is in these pages in ways that no one is likely ever to grasp.

It is not quite enough to say that Pete Sanders at PCCS Books has my gratitude yet again for giving me a platform for my thoughts and the opportunity to connect with more than a few close friends and colleagues. There is a phrase in Tagalog for the kind of gratitude I feel towards Pete: *utang na loob*. Translated loosely, it is an inner sense of debt, a debt of gratitude that cannot be quantified.

The commissioning editor at PCCS Books, Catherine Jackson, also has my sincere thanks, beginning with my appreciation of her clear and insightful feedback on my initial proposal. Her feedback helped to shape this project correctly from the beginning. Her input brought a focus that allowed my ideas to flow into the chapters you are holding. My thanks also to the entire staff at PCCS Books, whose work at every level allowed this book to reach you.

Special thanks to my readers, three extraordinary role models I am lucky enough to call my friends: Carol Wolter-Gustafson, Faith Kaplan and Marge Witty. Carol welcomed me into her home after reading my draft. She lovingly went over my manuscript with me for hours, page by page, at her dining-room table. Faith, true to her nature, did not just read my words but deeply integrated what she read into her thinking and regularly brought this understanding into conversations with me. Marge, one of my favourite warriors and co-conspirators over the years, also read my draft lovingly and gave me her unique and powerful perspective.

I have been fortunate to publish three books in the last 15 years or so. I do not think it is a coincidence that, over that time, I have been working closely with Ron and Faith Kaplan. They are mentors, colleagues and friends who have a unique gift for creating spaces that free people to pursue what inspires and excites them. They make continued growth not only possible but fun.

And, of course, my gratitude goes to you for reading this. Thank you for your curiosity and your willingness to let my words into your mind and for giving my thoughts some consideration.

Oakville, Ontario, 2019

Introduction

This is an act of hope: every recorded story implies a future reader.
Margaret Atwood (2017: xvii)

This book began with a single question: what gets in the way of understanding other people? That one question took hold in me many years ago. It drove an internal dialogue that has accompanied me throughout my professional journey and has found its way into the pages that follow. Stepping back and looking at my work over the last 25 years, the common factor in what I do is encountering people. It doesn't matter whether I encounter other people in therapy, legal assessment, supervision or some other form of work, I always find myself facing another human being who is looking for help, looking to be understood, or looking for answers to questions. What is the best way to face people, listen to and hear them? What gets in the way of understanding people? As answers opened up to me, they brought more questions, and those questions brought more answers, which coalesced around themes. Those themes grew into chapters and gave life to this book, which in the end may offer more questions than answers. If you are looking for the latest research or for concrete answers to apply immediately in your work with other people, you likely have come to the wrong place. I am happy for you to be here, of course, but if you stay you are more likely to find questions.

Nonetheless, I hope to make this book personal and to connect with something essential in you that may welcome the questions that come. It is in this spirit that I offer you an invitation: I hope you will come in and feel comfortable enough to stay for a while.

This book is many things. It carries my understanding of the field I love and that I have lived, worked and played in for the better part of 25 years. It is a personal reflection of how I understand my work with other people as a psychologist. It is a steady stream of questions that may lead to seeing the people we work with more fully for who they are. It holds my thoughts about the belief systems that underpin all that we do. It holds my experiences and reflections with respect to our devices and methods, from personality theory to diagnosis and the dominant tools of psychological testing and interviewing. It is increasingly personal, eventually leading the reader through my thoughts on what it means to us as human beings to work within and be affected by systems, and the impact of power and our fears. It is an alternative to textbooks on clinical psychology. It is a work of critical psychology, asking questions about the bases of our field and what we do. It is a book that holds my ideas and thoughts for young practitioners seeking an alternative source of supervision and study, and it is a book for more seasoned practitioners who may be thinking about what they are really doing after all these years of working with other people.

I wrote this book with a clear, increasingly personal progression in mind, chapter by chapter. The order of the chapters has meaning, and I believe each chapter has more meaning coming on the heels of the chapters that precede it. I begin by questioning reality – at least, the reality we each think exists – and suggesting that we question everything, including science. I offer an exploration of the Newtonian science with which our field has merged, which I see as a devolution in our approach to understanding people. In the shadow of this, I explore what was lost when we stopped paying attention to more modern understandings of physics as a scientific model that informs our field. I question the pillars of psychology: diagnosis, personality theory and psychological testing, and I also question language itself. As the chapters become increasingly personal, the questioning turns to a focus on ourselves: how systems influence us, how power influences us, and how fear influences us.

If I had to summarise all of the themes I explore and the questions I raise, I would arrive at the importance of questioning everything and learning to let things go in order to see people better. So why write an entire book if that is all I really want to get across? Sometimes I am not certain, to be honest. I have had plenty of moments when I asked myself why I should put any of this down on paper; when I questioned whether I had anything new or meaningful to offer when so much has been written in our field already. But I think we learn from telling each other stories and, after a few decades in the field, I have some stories to tell. Even if the message is simple, sometimes a story will carry it better. That is my hope, at least.

A brief note on terminology. Carl Rogers took us from the notion of patient to client and then, further, to person. I have avoided using the words 'patient' and 'client', except where those words are explicitly used in the context of another person's view. This book is not about patients or clients. It is about people – the people we face in our work, and it is also about you and me. This book is a meditation on what keeps us from encountering people more fully in our work. It is a reflection on what we do in our field with and to other people and how we may dehumanise them and fail to see them for who they are. Here I am further inspired and find strength in these words from a person who survived torture:

> The most important thing is that they treat you as a person. Don't treat the person as a client or service user or whatever people choose to call us. Treat them like a person, and when they come to see you, be personable. (Kakooza, 2017: 108)

On a personal note, it is somewhat frustrating for me to find it necessary to state that I am a scientist – to have to make it clear that I am not abandoning science and that I recognise its value. I'm trained as a scientist; to be regulated as a practitioner in the field, I had to pass examinations and be recognised by my peers for my grasp of the science of our field. My work is influenced by science, but it is also influenced by ethics, religion and art. I see my work as a psychologist as, in many ways, reclaiming the fullness of our field, including an appreciation of subjective 'data', and the art of gathering it well – the art of knowing another person. At the same time, this book challenges the subjective as much as the objective. Nothing is safe from questioning.

As I found myself fairly far into the process of writing this book, going down various avenues and back alleys, I realised this book is also about how our attitudes towards the work we do and the people we do it with are shaped, and how we can examine these attitudes. For everyone who has ever asked how an attitudes-based approach to working with people can be taught, this book is my personal answer. This is one place to start.

And so, with a certain sense of vulnerability mixed with hopefulness, I recognise that it is time to commit myself to print in the chapters that follow. Once these words are printed, they will live their own life, and my life then will go in whatever direction it goes, as will my thinking. I have strung together around 60,000 words in a more or less coherent fashion. If even 60 of them inspire you and find their way into your thinking, I will consider this book a great success. My hope is that my words will reach you and take root. I hope they will grow and flower into countless questions, filling your inner world with colours that you and I have not yet imagined.

References

Atwood M (1985/2017). *The Handmaid's Tale.* Toronto: Penguin Random House Canada.

Kakooza P (2017). Treat us like people. In: Boyles J (ed). *Psychological Therapies for Survivors of Torture: a human-rights approach with people seeking asylum.* Monmouth: PCCS Books (pp97–108).

Part 1

Science is dead

1
Life-giver

Every single one of us goes through life depending on and being bound by our individual knowledge and awareness. And we call it reality.
Itachi Uchiha (Kishimoto, 2016: 104)

We often prefer statements to questions. They are more comforting, solid, stable. We can settle into them and make our homes there. Life is simpler when we know what to expect and what to do, when we are certain of how to see things. Questions, on the other hand, require a nomadic existence, a life of change and ambiguity. When questions become our home, we have to trust our ability to survive the changes they may bring. Sometimes facing that change is very uncomfortable. What will it mean to give up something that seemed so certain and solid? Will it be OK? Will I be OK? Will I lose myself? As a child, I wanted to know such things as why the sky is blue, why the sun and moon don't fall or float away, where babies come from and why we all die. I also came to understand that questions are a part of my cultural inheritance as a Jew. Why start the day with nightfall? Why is this night different from all other nights? Always 'Why?' I generally find that answers lead me to more questions and a greater sense of wonder. Asking questions is how I orient to life.

Stating that life is a mystery is as unoriginal as it is obvious. Through the ages, artists, philosophers, scientists and sages have grappled with fundamental questions that many of us also have struggled with at one time or another. What is the meaning of life? Why are we here? What is our purpose? For me, a more compelling question is how do we make sense of reality? Whether or not we ask questions to orient to the world, we come into a world of abundant stimulation and must learn how to adapt and relate to it, to make sense of reality. We join others who are already here, and we tend to trust them and the reality they teach us, directly and indirectly. We do this before we even have words. Others shape our behaviours and our basic understanding of right and wrong, good and bad. Knowingly or not, we learn the world through those who raise and surround us, in ever-increasing webs of social and cultural complexity.

Woven into the fabric of our social world are family, ethnic, linguistic, regional and national influences. Belief systems are also handed down over generations, and they may transcend all of these influences. They help to give us containers for the world, to simplify it and navigate it. Belief systems offer us ways of thinking and understanding that are accepted on a grand scale by vast multitudes of people as explanatory systems for the world around us. They influence how we behave, how we see ourselves and how we see what is happening around us. They give us certainty and security – thinking that we know reality and that we share this understanding with those around us. Religion and science are among the most influential belief systems. Perhaps you are familiar with them.

Belief systems are so powerful, so compelling, so entrenched that we may have no idea we are held in their thrall. At some point we may begin to mistake a belief system itself for reality and defend it vigorously, while perhaps also denigrating other belief systems that may not seem to fit well for us. A belief system is vast and complex and seems to explain so much. We may see many people around us who seem to agree that this belief system explains reality. And we may respect them highly, reinforcing our belief that we arrive at the truth by seeing things through a particular belief system. There are experts in these belief systems, whose knowledge of the system is so immense that we also may feel intimidated. We may feel we could never understand so much, even after a lifetime of study.

And so we may give our authority over to others, eagerly feed on their knowledge and make it our own, without serious question. These figures can seem like titans. Many are truly giants among thinkers. Long before we were born or could form words, they have already shaped the words of the language we are born into and will come to learn, building solid fortresses that house a particular belief system. They may even be worshipped to some degree. Who are we to question? It becomes easier to accept it, to follow it, to get to know our world through this unquestioned lens. We may even call our unquestioning deference 'respect'.

Yet this is where thinking and life end, when a belief system is swallowed whole and goes unquestioned, and perhaps even unrecognised. In this way, a belief system quietly shapes how we listen and think and the opinions and conclusions we form. The system itself and its products become reified. This is especially powerful when the belief system becomes the assumed world view of most people around us. In order to question a belief system and to see the world less narrowly, we have to first recognise that we have been co-opted, that we operate within a belief system, and that it gives us only a very small sense of the reality that lies beyond it. In order to see people more clearly, it may be necessary at times to challenge our belief systems. In an increasingly secular world, it may be easiest to challenge religion, even to mock it. Science stands tall in our modern world and appears unassailable. But science, too, is not beyond questioning. A belief system that cannot be questioned, and perhaps even mocked, is likely a dead one.

For many of us, our earliest learning is religious, though we are increasingly raised on science. Some of us are old enough and lucky enough to have grown up with the joy of watching Carl Sagan's *Cosmos* when it first aired on public television, his voice full of wonder as he explained the nature of the universe through the lens of science. He opened my mind to the magical and wondrous idea that we are all star stuff – exploded stars that are now looking back at ourselves across time and trying to understand where we come from, what we are and where we are going.

Even as science strengthens its hold, religion is nonetheless all around us. Whether at home, in a place of worship or indirectly, as part of a larger society overflowing with religious images and messages, religion finds its way into our minds, bidden or not. I recall Bible stories as being among the earliest stories I heard. These stories still lead me to continual questioning. The stories of *Bereishit*, which in Hebrew means 'to begin with...', are some of the most well-known stories in the world, with metaphors that can unfold and become richer over time. Chances are you know these as the stories of *Genesis*. Unfortunately, they also can be understood concretely, and this is often the case, especially when we don't take the time or find the interest to engage with them. They have the power to guide us, limit us or turn us off entirely, depending on how we relate to them.

I am not a Bible scholar and, depending on who you ask, I may be seen as an atheist, regardless of how I see myself. From my perspective, I am just a Jew who loves to ask questions – questions upon questions. I am uncomfortable when questions are not permitted. An ancient story from *Bereishit* comes to mind that captures the tension between questioning and remaining in the paradise of ignorance that comes from not questioning: the story of Havva and Adam. In our Christian-centric world, we may view this story in a rigid way, especially given our familiarity with it. Even my describing it as the story of Havva and Adam may be jarring to some readers who are more familiar with calling it the story of Adam and Eve.

Havva and Adam live in a paradise that God made for them. God set out one rule, which actually seems quite simple: don't eat from that tree. That tree was the tree of the knowledge of good and evil. Certainly having this knowledge would lead one to question some things. Most of us understand that a serpent tempted Havva to eat the tree's fruit, and she then tempted Adam. When God finds out, they are supposedly punished for the sin of disobedience and sent out of paradise to live a life in which they will know pain and death. As a secular Jew in a Christian world, it is a challenge for me to see beyond the Christian telling of my ancestors' stories and to question them properly. But questioning our ancient texts is, in part, what reveals their sacred quality – they don't break when questioned; rather, they become a source of nourishment, a belief system with life in it, and yes, even star stuff.

What if the story of Havva and Adam were not about sin? Havva and Adam were commanded not to act on the temptation to seek knowledge. And, according to the story, God put the tree in the garden purposely, pointed it out to them and told them it was dangerous. Of course they would eat from it! What do you think happens when a young person sees an adult content warning appear before a TV show saying it is not suitable for young viewers, or when someone under 18 years of age sees a website that says you must be over 18 to enter? Are you over 18? Yes? No?

What if Havva was actually courageous in her questioning of the rules? If Havva had not initiated this bold act, the *Tanakh* (*Torah*, *Prophets* and the *Writings*) would not unfold with its ultimate vision of a world beyond politics. She and Adam would still be spending eternity following the rules in 'paradise' and not experiencing any challenge, change or growth. They would have remained in a so-called paradise where nothing is questioned. All is given, as long as one rule is followed: don't be tempted by knowledge. With Havva's courageous act of questioning authority, the human story actually begins in full. We are beings who struggle with conflicting feelings and thoughts, who know joy and pain. It is not necessary to see our nature as being the result of a sin – it is simply who we are, the nature of being human. Perhaps we are too confined by sexism, along with the Christian yoke, to see this woman's true courage and power – to see that Havva is our first true hero. Havva was the thinker, the revolutionary, and Adam the follower.

The creation story itself presents a frame that questions the accepted order of things: a single day begins with the night and enters into light. The day does not begin when the sun rises or when our alarm clock rudely wakes us from the joy of sleep. This theme of turning things on their head, questioning everything, even questioning God, runs throughout the *Torah*, the *Prophets*, and the *Writings*. For me it is an essential part of what makes ancient scripture come alive. I find that the theme of questioning is most profoundly explored in this first human story in *Bereishit*, which we often call 'The Fall'. From this perspective, we tell this story as an explanation of when and how our problems began as humans.

Perhaps it would be more appropriate to see this story as 'The Rise', as this is when the human story begins, by asking questions, seeking out knowledge and not being content to simply follow authority. What if, instead of a tragic expulsion from paradise, this story is actually about when our potential for freedom began, and Havva led the way? Perhaps Havva and Adam were not punished, or at least not for 'sinning'. Adam calls the first woman 'Havva', life-giver, *after* they learn of the consequences of their actions. Perhaps they simply take on the consequences of thinking for themselves, the consequences of the actions they take without depending on the rules set down by others. By living and questioning, they will inevitably sacrifice comfort, experience pain and take responsibility for their actions. But that is actually alright. It is called being an adult. And perhaps the God of

Bereishit knew his children had to grow up; God knew they would want to eat the fruit, to know things and question, and made sure they knew where to find it. He even made sure his children had clothes when they left home, to protect them and keep them warm as they made their way in the outside world.

If Havva had not been courageous, this would have been the *Torah* story: 'Meanwhile, back in the Garden, it is pretty much all the same and always will be. Today is like yesterday and tomorrow will be like today.' No change, no stories, no struggles, no births, no deaths, no triumphs, no pain, and probably also no true joy, which exists because of the contrast with also knowing pain. Just sameness, lack of responsibility and initiative – total, blissful dependence. The *Genesis* story would end if it were not for Havva's questioning. No need for wisdom to be passed down. No need to tell stories, no need to study, no need to understand. The end. And no one would have been around to read this very short story, other than Havva and Adam, who had no need to read.

Maybe ignorance really is bliss, but I can't fathom a world without questions. Abraham argues with God in an effort to prevent the destruction of a city. Moses also famously questions God. But Havva questions and acts. She is willing to face death for a life with the freedom to think for herself and to act independently. She rebels through questioning. But this rebellion is not for the sake of being disobedient or oppositional; rather, it is for knowledge. Havva rebels to understand, and in so doing she changes the course of human history. The genesis of life lies within asking questions. Questioning is the fundamental act that allows us to begin to understand, and I believe Havva was trying to understand, to reach for knowledge. Understanding what lies beyond ourselves and beyond where we are comfortable is the beginning of real empathy. When we ask questions to understand other people, we, too, may find ourselves having to give up the comfort of our own reality to embrace a reality that lies beyond our idyllic garden.

I know this interpretation may be uncomfortable to hear, let alone accept. But these themes reverberate throughout the ancient Jewish scriptures, including the words and acts of the prophets. This first human story is about the choice to question and break free from rules. Havva quite literally did not give birth to life until she was no longer in the garden. Her name, Havva (life-giver), to me means more than being the first mother to us all, but the mother to truly being alive, giving us the possibility of freedom. You might say, 'Wait a minute! That's not right! That's not the story I was taught!' You might even see my interpretation and questioning of this story as a blasphemy, depending on your view of the world. It may make no sense to you; you may simply see it as wrong. Or maybe science is your belief system, to the exclusion of religion. You may have such a strong reaction to religion as a belief system that you shut down and do not listen because your mind is made up. And that is my point. That is the power of a belief system that goes unquestioned or unexplored because we think we already know it. Questioning it, whether or not you are satisfied with the answers, can open up new ways of thinking and seeing within you.

We now live in a largely secular world, and many of us write off these stories as quaint tales at best, or stories of oppression at worst. So, back to not questioning. We are all, for the most part, born into gardens we don't question. Not questioning drains the life from a belief system and leaves it dead. Religious groups often adhere strictly to rules and the need for one interpretation – a paradise of sorts in which ignorance is supposedly bliss and imposed on all. Questions are not allowed in paradise. It is this dogma, this lifeless orthodoxy, that ruled Europe when a man named Galileo Galilei began to look at things around him and ask some questions. He looked for life beyond the deadened world of the orthodoxy around him, and he was seen as a heretic. During his time, dogma held that the earth was the centre of the universe, along with a number of other beliefs that were dangerous to challenge. Pursuing knowledge that challenged dogma could lead to death: a pretty dangerous truth to pursue. Religion, and Christianity in particular, was the dominant source of truth across Europe. But Galileo looked through his telescope and made observations that did not fit dogma. He came to understand that the earth is not the centre of the universe and the sun and planets do not revolve around us. He observed something that challenged the dominant belief system, and those who represented that belief system were perhaps threatened and afraid. They were inflexible and punished him for speaking up.

Galileo was the Havva of his time. He was tempted by knowledge, and his questions ultimately turned Europe upside down and led to the rapid emergence of a powerful new belief system: science. Science introduced a new way of understanding the world. Theories are developed and challenged through observing, gathering information in a systematic way and asking whether or not this information supports theory. Experiments are carefully designed to test or challenge theories, and they are carried out repeatedly. When data don't support a theory, the theory falls and a new theory may develop. Science holds within it an endless process of questioning – not only questioning our views of the world but questioning the current state of our scientific understanding.

In today's world, where science has risen to prominence over religion as a belief system, it may be difficult to rush headlong into questioning its limits. Since Galileo's brave statements, born from his observations of the world and the worlds beyond us in the night sky, science has steadily taken hold as a powerful belief system, pushing religion further and further from a place of relevance for many. With the rise of science, many are now able to recognise and objectively examine the dominant belief system of religion. With the comfort and power of belonging to a world that increasingly values science over religion, it becomes easier to be critical of religious belief systems, to question their relevance as explanatory models, and to see more possibilities beyond religion. Unfortunately, it can also result in becoming so over-identified with science that religion is easily and too quickly ridiculed and discounted. Understanding religion as a belief system that can still be relevant is lost in an either-or, us-versus-them struggle. And science, like any belief system, may carry within it the seeds of earlier belief systems. It is just as vulnerable to the human tendency to create an orthodoxy and to reify that system, rather than stay open to ambiguity and questions. Indeed, as Havelock Ellis wrote almost 100 years ago, in *The Dance of Life*:

> Matter is a fiction, just as the fundamental ideas with which the sciences generally operate are mostly fictions, and the scientific materialisation of the world has proved a necessary and useful fiction, only harmful when we regard it as hypothesis and therefore possibly true. The representative world is a system of fictions. It is a symbol by the help of which we orient ourselves. The business of science is to make the symbol ever more adequate, but it remains a symbol, a means of action, for action is the last end of thinking. (1923: 97)

In other words, belief systems themselves are not real, but always point to something beyond them. Our mistake is to make them real and believe wholeheartedly in those realities we have created simply to help us think about things and try to understand and find our way in the world. Given the power that science now enjoys, Galileo's act of giving voice to his observations that challenged the previously dominant belief system may not be seen readily for the radical and dangerous act it actually was. It is possible now to see even more clearly why Galileo was so threatening – he was largely alone in offering an alternative to the prevailing belief system. This is, interestingly, what we face now if we question science. Any views that are not obviously scientific are written off as soft. Ironically, they may even be described by some as heretical. If we challenge a view or statement that appears to be steeped in science, we run the risk of being branded heretics. To be a clinician accused of not being scientific is a fate many of us strive to avoid.

Although religion is still powerful, science arguably has become the central source of truth for many, especially in the field of psychology. Science has become a belief system so big and powerful that it may not even be seen as such and appears to be beyond questioning. Picasso is credited with once saying that painting is a lie that tells the truth. When misused or adhered to blindly, science is a truth that tells a lie. And for many, that is a very hard pill to swallow – that science may not hold all the answers, or that science might hold answers that mislead and misdirect us.

Science presents a new potential for tyranny, and the products of the scientific method can go unquestioned. This is perhaps ironic, since science is a system of questioning. However, those questions can be misleading because of the tools we have to answer them, or because of the limitations in the very questions we pose. A tendency to gravitate towards the more concrete can also lead us astray when we interpret our findings. Much of what I explore in the next chapters is a reflection of the various ways scientific pronouncements and findings can fall short of offering a fuller truth and sometimes can cause great harm by masquerading as a truth that does not fit the human reality it was meant to somehow summarise. Science does not answer everything and does not hold the only truths, or perhaps even the most meaningful or fullest truths. Even a so-called theory of everything does not explain everything.

At the same time, great belief systems also have something important to offer. I am not advocating for their destruction when I advocate for questioning. Every belief system offers a unique lens that can contribute to how we see the world and other people. Discounting religion, for example, means neglecting such great thinkers as Maimonides, whose medical ethics sprang from deep spiritual devotion and study. It means ignoring the rich intellectual and personal growth that comes from questioning, interpreting and even debating *Torah*. Likewise, discounting science means neglecting a powerful check on our blind spots and assumptions – we can observe that the earth revolves around the sun and then reflect on what this means about how we see ourselves and others and our place in the universe. Scientists can ask wonderful questions that stretch our imaginations.

What we learn shapes how we see, and this becomes a trap we may not be able to see beyond. Science actually helps us to know we are wired this way. Contemporary neuroscience reveals that emotions actually play a critical role in rational thought (Damasio, 1994). It also reveals that we create our emotions and that our personal emotions are actually not universal. According to Lisa Feldman Barrett, 'variation is the norm. Emotion fingerprints are a myth' (2017: 23). In other words, emotions are as individual as we are. Our understanding of our facts and experiences may change, sometimes uncomfortably, as we come across new facts. Carl Rogers once said, 'The facts are friendly' (1961: 25). My concern is that the facts may be a little too friendly, perhaps seductive, and may sometimes blind us from seeing the context around them. Fortunately, the scientific method itself suggests continual questioning, offering a way to break free from the seductiveness of the facts, a way to open our eyes, a way to shatter dangerous orthodoxies and dogmas. Just like ancient spiritual wisdom, science won't break if we question it, explore what its limits are and reconsider how it fits with other ways of seeing and being.

Because I am publicly questioning science, or at least how we sometimes use it, it would be easy to give in to fear and write this book in some other way, or perhaps not write it at all. I am reminded, of course, of Freud's work. What if he had drawn upon Hebrew source stories instead of Greek, as I have done here? Would Sigmund Freud, born Sigismund Schlomo Freud, have reached his non-Jewish Austrian audience, the dominant culture he assimilated to? Would he have put himself or others in grave danger? His last work, *Moses and Monotheism* (1967), reveals that he was acutely aware of these dangers.

My present situation does not appear to be as immediately dangerous as Freud's, nor as dangerous as Galileo's. Nonetheless, I question science here with some trepidation about the potential consequences. I do it because I know it is the right thing to do when I see that adhering to a narrow view of science gets in the way of seeing another person more fully. I accept, uncomfortably, there may be consequences. However, seeing another person is more important to me, a more worthy act than adhering blindly or rigidly to a belief system for the sake of that system and my identification with it.

There are many ways of looking at the world and trying to understand ourselves and other people. Reality is necessarily limited by our filters: senses, perceptions, unchallenged beliefs, theories, culture, ethnicity and language. These shape our truths, our thinking and how we observe and think about what we have observed. If we then use only one belief system as a lens to view the world, we are unnecessarily restricted. It is important to recognise when one is blindly and exclusively following a belief system. Such a rigid perspective is likely to interfere with information that can come readily and more directly through experience and other sources of knowing.

Strict adherence to a belief system can interfere with our humility and our ability to see what is right in front of us. We rarely question our culture or ethnicity, the books we read, the information we are bombarded with and the way our language and the aesthetic of what is around us shapes our reality. Beyond this, our own experience and the experiences of other people are uniquely complex and individual. They are powerful ways of knowing. And what are knowledge and knowing without wonder, awe and respect, without the humility of recognising our own uniquely complex identities as sources of influence on the answers we come to? Recognition of all that goes into us, and how that unique and infinitely diverse mix shapes our view of other people, is an ongoing challenge.

A first step towards seeing other people more fully is recognising our belief systems for what they are, appreciating and valuing what may be useful about them, and not being bound by them. Confronting science is as good a place as any to start. I believe that, wherever psychology rigidly applies science without encountering the other person and asking questions, science is dead. Questioning is the ultimate life-giver. We each live in our own Eden, and I recommend eating some forbidden fruit. Ask a question.

References

Barrett LF (2017). *How Emotions Are Made: the secret life of the brain*. Boston, MA: Mariner Books.

Damasio A (1994). *Descartes' Error: emotion, reason, and the human brain*. New York, NY: Penguin Books.

Ellis H (1923). *The Dance of Life*. Boston, MA: Houghton Mifflin Company.

Freud S (1967). *Moses and Monotheism*. New York, NY: Vintage Books.

Kishimoto M (2016). *Naurto, volume 42* (Shonen Jump Manga edition). San Francisco, CA: VIZ Media.

Rogers CR (1961). *On Becoming a Person: a therapist's view of psychotherapy*. Boston, MA: Houghton Mifflin Company.

2

Misalignment

the maps they gave us were out of date by years
Adrienne Rich (1978: 31)

I entered my undergraduate studies as an engineering student. Back then, I could lose myself happily while trying to solve a calculus problem in the engineering library on a Friday night. Eternal geek. Unfortunately, I found out there was relatively little opportunity to take elective coursework in the humanities. And, as much as I love science, I also love the humanities. Perhaps I could have done a better job of reading the curriculum guide in advance of declaring my major, and then I would have been less surprised by the road ahead. Perhaps. Nevertheless, because of the specialised nature of engineering studies, it felt like I had become a graduate student as an undergraduate. The engineering major only allowed for one elective outside of engineering studies each year. That did not hold a great deal of appeal for me because I wanted to study history, religion, languages, art and literature. I was not quite ready to give up on that, and it did not take long to discover that one elective a year would not be enough to satisfy me.

Science is simply not enough for me, despite the many wonders it holds. My one elective during my first year as an engineering major was 'Introduction to Psychology', and that was all it took. I was hooked. I ultimately soaked up 18 courses in psychology as an undergraduate, even staying for summer school because I wanted to take more. I was first drawn to the field because it is a mix of so many fascinating fields, all in the context of attempting to understand what it means to be human: art, music, literature, philosophy, linguistics, ethics, politics, history, religion and, of course, science. I find that when I immerse myself in any of these, I am studying what it means to be human, and hopefully becoming a better psychologist. As a psychologist, I see myself as a student of individual differences and realities. I see my field everywhere I go, and in all that I experience. This complex mix has remained an enduring fascination.

My path through the field of psychology since my undergraduate years has been circuitous, and I have often found myself working in settings I never would have imagined. My unexpected journey began when I rejected a number of scholarship offers to study experimental psychology at the doctoral level, which quickly led to a significant period of unemployment and an important lesson in humility. Since then, I have trained or worked in hospitals and psychiatric facilities, workshops for people with developmental disabilities, chronic care facilities, university and private counselling centres and various private practice settings. My experience as a psychologist over the last 25 years or so in these settings has been heavily weighted towards assessment and treatment. Currently, my practice also includes assessment work for legal purposes, and occasionally I end up testifying about my understanding of an individual in trials, arbitrations and tribunals. Over the last decade and a half, I have also been involved in advocacy work, attempting to educate the government, insurers, lawyers and health professionals about what we do as psychologists and the impact of legislation on the people we see in our work.

It is fair to say that science is an important factor in all of the areas I am engaged in as a part of my practice. Indeed, we psychologists generally present ourselves to others as scientists. We seem to be most readily heard and respected when we speak from this perspective. Even when we present ourselves as clinicians, we often say that we are clinician-scientists. I was formally trained as a clinician-scientist, as were most of my colleagues. I also had the good fortune to connect with a group of wonderfully odd practitioners working out of Carl Rogers' counselling centre in Chicago. They regularly thought outside the box, and discussions around ethics, politics, and power in the context of our work had a happy and comfortable home there. It was there that I first felt complete freedom to question everything I do as a psychologist, including the role played by science.

The scientific method involves gathering data to explore our questions. It is applied by human beings, with all of our lenses and biases, known and unknown to us. The questions we ask, the tools we use and the data we gather may shape our answers in ways that mislead us. The complexity is then compounded when we apply our science to individual human beings. The danger when we do this is that we narrow our appreciation of the other person's experience and the impact of our relationship, as well as the impact of our experience, on our ability to see them.

Bodies of scientific research, like the individuals who build them, are vulnerable to developing unchecked biases. The peer review approach to the publication of articles in research journals is meant to be a check on quality to prevent junk science. This is, of course, a good thing. However, it may be difficult for new voices, innovative researchers, to break through and be heard because of the questions their research raises. These questions may challenge the life's work of the reviewers, who are often well-established researchers.

Research findings also take on a certain power because of the way we give science authority without questioning it. Asking questions, pulling back for the broader human context, can be neglected when we hold narrowly to concrete findings in a research study. Large questions may go unanswered, such as the impact we have on other people when we apply techniques in order to change them. What is it that actually changes? What are someone's reasons or motivations for faking or exaggerating symptoms when tested or interviewed? Have we actually gathered enough information to really understand someone by using a structured interview? Have we found truth, and if so, whose truth is it? What exactly are we doing with our science, and how are we understanding its products and the measurements we are taking?

It is important to remind ourselves that the scientific method is a systematic method for continually asking questions to arrive at answers that are reliable. We lose sight of the importance of questioning. We hold fast to the products or data that our method generates. We forget the limits of the tools we use for measuring and our infinite capacity for fooling ourselves into believing that the results mean only one thing. Thus, the products of our research and the data yielded by our clinical work can become lies we believe because we believe firmly in science and the scientific method. It is easy to do. It is seductive.

Psychology is fundamentally an insecure field – or, perhaps more accurately, a field that includes a number of practitioners who may feel insecure. This is, of course, unfortunate, but it is also understandable. We internalise the messages we hear all around us. How often have I heard, 'All you do is listen to people,' or, even better, 'How is talking to you any different from talking to my cat?' I have also heard, 'But you aren't a real doctor, are you?' and this question has found its way indirectly or directly into cross-examinations I have faced in legal settings. It is when these messages tap into our own insecurities that we are lost. All too often, we lose sight of the great value we offer in our efforts to see people more fully in the activities we carry out in our clinical work.

Insecurity leaves us vulnerable to the influence of a cult mindset, and a blind adherence to science has become a cult for many psychologists. Science is given a central place of worship in our view of humanity. In order to maintain our sense of self-worth and dignity, we may have a great deal invested in being seen as good scientists, good believers. We believe in science. We are regarded highly simply because we show that we are using science, and we find strength and comfort in numbers, in belonging to a field aligned with science. Ironically, this alignment undermines our science and kills it. There are pressures to be seen as good scientists, and these can influence how we understand our work and other people. This is especially true depending on the model of science we are influenced by and how firmly we keep other belief systems out of our attempts at understanding other people and ourselves. I am not suggesting that psychology should abandon science. Far from it; I love my field, including our science. That is why I question it. I believe there is no need to pretend to be anything or to announce loudly that we are a certain thing while ignoring the rest of what we are. Perhaps when we come to recognise fully the value of what we do, we will be able to let go of having to adhere so closely to one belief system.

Everything I study and experience impacts on my work and my attempts to understand other people: reading ancient spiritual texts, meditating on poetry, listening to a classical music performance, chatting with friends and family, watching my dog sleep, watching anime, tending my garden and watching the seasons change, or reading a novel at bedtime. Science can take on a commanding, almost suffocating role at the expense of these other ways of seeing and being. The subjective is too readily diminished, and the skill of hearing it fully is too easily lost in the process.

However, it seems that the questions others ask us, the questions that challenge us and our insecurities, may push us further into an obsession with science as the only way to be seen as credible and to have value in the eyes of others. Thus we put enormous energy into our research studies, the development of tests to predict behaviour and describe people, the creation of cookie-cutter interview formats to gather information, the design of manualised techniques and approaches to apply to other people in an effort to change them, and the refinement of a diagnostic system to classify people for research and selecting empirically supported treatments to apply to them. Power comes with this, as not everyone is allowed by law to diagnose or, by extension, to interpret psychological tests. Science has its privileges, and among them is the sense of comfort that comes with being regarded highly in society.

Psychology has been a home for many good scientists. We even have our fair share of great scientists. One of these was Carl Rogers. His name is synonymous with the person-centred approach, which was a significant part of my training and remains a powerful influence on my work. To other psychologists, that means something. Usually it means I must be a soft-minded psychologist; I must not be very serious about what I do. Over the years, I have lived with this easy denigration of a central aspect of my orientation and my work. Sadly, Rogers' careful, scientific study of the factors that support growth in a relationship are all but ignored. His understanding of the role that values play in being with and listening to another person seems largely forgotten. Even his bold step of releasing audio recordings of sessions is no longer widely known. He was the first.

Outside our field, the neurologist Sigmund Freud is probably the most known and influential figure in popular culture conceptions of psychology, although psychologists have also denigrated his ideas. This is, in part, due to misunderstanding and discomfort over the kinds of truth he was expressing. Both Rogers and Freud said some very threatening things. Rogers discussed an approach to being with other people based on the ethical stance of giving up power over others and trusting them. Freud openly discussed our aggressive and sexual impulses and directly asserted that we are not aware of most of what is happening within us. I admit to having a soft spot for RD Laing (1990), who took Freud a step further and said we are all murderers and prostitutes. Or, as Margaret Atwood wrote so poetically in *The Handmaid's Tale*: 'The crimes of others are a secret language among us. Through them we show ourselves what we might be capable of, after all' (1985/2017: 316–317).

Either line of thinking, Rogerian or Freudian, leads to difficult self-reflection, and sometimes having to challenge and give up cherished views of ourselves. Given our rather commonplace insecurities, it is not surprising that neither approach remains popular. On the other hand, an empirically based, data-driven approach that relies on numbers and statistics does not require any messy, uncomfortable or time-consuming self-reflection. It can bypass and conveniently shut down the messy, uncomfortable and seemingly rude Rogerian or Freudian discourse. And it often does. That is why, within the field, it seems to me that the psychologist who probably had the most influence on our present state is Paul Meehl. His 1954 book, *Clinical Versus Statistical Prediction* (1954/2013), may be the single most influential work in our field today, even if you have not heard of it.

This thin, unassuming volume laid the groundwork for the dominance of an objective, basically Newtonian, conception of human beings – for a trust in numbers, 'hard' objective data, over our own 'soft' perceptions and subjective sources of data. Meehl's book set up an either/or scenario. The title plainly states it: *Clinical Versus Statistical Prediction*. There is no embracing of a both/and in this title. And many in the field have followed him, dutifully, happily, comfortably. We are all scientists after all. Even the use of the word 'prediction', as opposed to 'understanding', in the title is an interesting choice. There is a subtle, or perhaps not, expression of the exercise of power over other people, the suggestion that we can use data to *predict* their lives, behaviours, thoughts and emotions in order to intervene and act on them. The subtitle is also telling: '*a theoretical analysis and a review of the evidence*'. It validates the title by making a plea to those of us who adhere to the belief system of science. Science will give us the answer. The data will tell us which one to choose. Yet what is hidden in plain sight is the false assumption that there must be a choice. Science does not actually prove or support a need for an either/or choice when it comes to appreciating the roles of objective and subjective information. But that is where psychology went.

Researchers in psychology use the scientific method. A variation of the scientific method is used in psychological assessment and we refer to it rather creatively as the psychological method. The psychological method is used for a variety of assessment purposes, such as designing treatment plans, determining disability or impairment levels, determining competence and exploring vocational options. This method is based on gathering information, which we call 'data', from multiple sources: reviewing healthcare records, interviewing the people we are working with and those who know them, behavioural observations and using psychological tests of symptom severity and cognitive functioning. When we employ this method, we weigh the information from all of these sources, look for convergences and divergences, and consider what hypothesis, explanation or story fits all of this information best. This is potentially a very powerful way of generating questions to arrive at satisfying answers, or unsatisfying answers we may have to learn to live with. It can be a slow, deliberate and complicated process to weigh all of these sources and consider how they do or do not fit together and what that might mean.

Unfortunately, the psychological method is now skewed heavily towards numbers, the 'objective' data. The influence of Paul Meehl's schism is everywhere. Even more unfortunately, the objective approach we have adopted is reductionist; it collapses the complexity of an individual human being in a Newtonian fashion. The idea, or perhaps dream, is that, with enough objective data from testing, we can answer questions about individuals and have an impact on them, much as we thought we could predict and perhaps even manipulate the universe if we had enough capacity to crank the massive collection of data describing it through Newton's formulas. The reality, when we wake up from our Newtonian dream, is that our lopsided reliance on numbers, the objective data, brings us no closer to the truth. As contemporary physicist Neil deGrasse Tyson has observed:

> To the scientist, the universality of physical laws makes the cosmos a marvelously simple place. By comparison, human nature – the psychologist's domain – is infinitely more daunting. (2017: 45)

There is nothing wrong with using a scientific lens in psychology. But if we want to be cutting-edge scientists, or at least to be seen as cutting-edge scientists, our frame, along with our techniques and practices, should reflect continuing developments in the sciences. So where is psychology as a science? What path have we taken? If we look at our field as it stands now, it is largely aligned with the work of Sir Isaac Newton, who was born in 1642. He published his ideas about how the universe works in his *Mathematical Principles of Natural Philosophy* in 1687 (1999), well over 300 years ago. His formulas have often been described as reducing the workings of the universe to a complex game of billiards, where cause always leads to effect. I would venture to say that there have been a few developments in the sciences since Newton's time, including Einstein's insights into special and general relativity and the emergence of quantum physics in the 20th century.

Physicists came to realise that they could not apply Newton's laws to all levels of observation in the universe. They even found that subjectivity plays an essential role, as we actually affect what we observe. Newtonian physics remains useful, but it certainly has its limits. Unfortunately, this is where psychologists are aligned as a field, reducing thoughts, feelings, behaviours and symptoms to numbers and conceptualising them as discrete objects. Welcome, gentle reader, to the age of Newtonian psychological technologies. Technologies arise out of the application of science, bringing it into the world for various uses. And in psychology these uses are applied to people. Newtonian psychology is not a thing of the distant past, and it is not emerging on the horizon. It is not someone's dystopian, science-fiction fantasy in which technology consumes our humanity and we all breathe a sigh of relief that it was just a novel, a story in a book. The pendulum has swung. The ship has sailed. It is real. It is here. We are living it now. We are playing billiards with individual lives.

Human experience is infinitely and wonderfully complex. It seems fairly obvious that there is something not quite right about reducing human experience, thoughts and feelings to operational variables that we act upon with our techniques. At the same time, there is no denying that there can be positive results. We know that Pavlov's dog salivated at the sound of a bell after the sound was repeatedly associated with food. The sound of that bell reinforced a new direction in our field. John Watson heard that bell and was inspired to undertake his experiment on emotionally healthy Little Albert. Watson 'conditioned' this child to be afraid of white rats. The experiment was so successful that Little Albert eventually came to fear all manner of white fluffy things, including cotton balls and Santa Claus and his beard. Token economies emerged as ways to shape behaviours in people diagnosed with schizophrenia or developmental disabilities. If you behave in a desired way, you get a token; after accumulating a certain number of tokens, you can exchange them for something you want. The psychological world soon became our Skinner Box; the possibilities for creating a utopia were endless.

The psychiatrist Aaron Beck and his cognitive therapy emerged from this brave new world. Beck observed that thoughts impact on emotions and behaviours, emotions impact on behaviours and thoughts, and behaviours impact on thoughts and emotions. Manipulate any one of this triad, the cause, and you arrive at a different effect. A psychological technology emerged to categorise the thoughts of the people we work with in an effort to change their emotions and behaviours, and then manuals were developed: put Tab A in Slot B. Cognitive behavioural therapy is now the dominant approach in our field. It is a perfect reductionist model for a game of billiards in Newton's universe.

Reductionism has even found its way into the person-centred approach in ways that are both subtle and grossly obvious. Some have used the person-centred approach and variations of it to effect change in other people – as a technique rather than a way of being. This can be seen in some efforts to train clinicians in how to listen. Listening is a critical aspect of our work. The obvious way to teach listening, scientifically, is to operationalise it – break it down, objectify it and make it into a technique for treatment. Some research into the person-centred approach has focused on the accuracy or quality of clinicians' listening by examining and quantifying their responses to the people they are listening to. I dislike this research because of the potential for clinicians to reify their understanding of empathic responses. Listening gets turned into a technique that uses empathic responses, rather than allowing empathic responses to emerge as a by-product of simply being fully present and trying to understand someone else from their perspective.

During my master's studies, I took an introductory course in 'counselling skills', based on the work of Robert Carkhuff. It was basically learning how to respond to the people we work with by using sentence stems: 'What I hear you saying is…, and you are feeling…' It was a course in robotic responding, and I hated it with a passion. Years later, I was part of a marathon person-centred group process. I remember disagreeing openly with someone and then hearing, 'I hear what you are saying, and I appreciate it.' I doubt I was actually heard, and I had the distinct feeling that what I said was not appreciated at all. As human beings, we are often exquisitely sensitive to canned responses and we tend not to appreciate them. Considering their impact, I believe that canned responses should remain in their cans and left out of our encounters with other people.

Newton's ideas may be more than 300 years old, but they are still useful, depending on the context. Cognitive behavioural therapy and other Newtonian psychological technologies have their place. The appeal is obvious. They can be manualised for treatment and easily operationalised for research. They are easy to teach and can be grasped readily by clinicians and the people we work with. Their concreteness has a certain appeal to some people. Many clinicians and the people they work with find these approaches a perfect fit. At the same time, many do not consider what is lost, and much has been lost in the tsunami of cognitive-behavioural reductionism that has torn through our field. There are limits to applying a manualised approach, applying technology, to human beings. We are not broken machines to be fixed by someone tinkering with us. We don't need to see mechanics for our emotional distress.

While I understand that clinicians have to start somewhere, being taught a canned technique may end up distracting us from relating more fully to another person who is suffering. Trying to figure out the right thing to say in response to another person, or fitting our responses to a template, is likely to get in the way of actually understanding them. Even focusing on what is a good or a bad empathic understanding response can get in the way of natural listening. I recall early experiences in group supervision, listening with fellow students to recordings of our therapy sessions. The feedback we gave each other was typically concrete and focused narrowly on the words spoken by the people we were working with, with suggestions for responses that might be more accurate. Responding to implied meanings was seen sometimes as getting ahead of the other person, rather than being empathic to implied meanings beyond the words or in the tone of voice carrying them, or to the body language that is also being expressed.

Our well-intentioned and sometimes eager feedback to each other added another potential barrier between us and our ability simply to be with another person and respond empathically. This approach sometimes reinforced that we must frequently say something in order to show our empathic understanding. It may also have reinforced the development of a response pattern that was closer to parroting, rather than one that flowed naturally from trying to understand someone. One student came to believe that the goal was to repeat back exactly what the other person said after every complete sentence they uttered.

In my experience, sometimes an empathic understanding response is as simple as having a focused presence, making appropriate eye contact, nodding the head, saying 'Mm-hmm' or asking a question to clarify and make sure we are following what the other person is saying. These responses come from a different place when they flow naturally from being attuned with full presence to another person, rather than consciously formulated and based on a technique. A therapist can be accurately and empathically understanding another person and say very little, and that person can still experience and receive this as having been listened to carefully and fully.

Psychology has produced a vast library of research studies. A lifetime is not nearly long enough to read it all. The Newtonian trend in our field has supported objective data – numbers – at the expense of subjective data – the lived experiences of the people we assess and treat. Our objective research leads to a manualised approach to therapy using empirically supported techniques, the construction of decision trees to follow for diagnostic interviewing and protocols for the use and interpretation of performance and symptom validity tests. Subjective information and context do not carry weight and are sometimes seen as little more than an afterthought; numbers and technology take centre stage.

I don't dismiss objective data; I simply want to know more. Objective data are an important source of information, but they are not always what they seem. When people are equated with statistics, we strip them of their individuality and fullness. It would be unfortunate to be aligned with only one way of seeing the world and apply it narrowly in our work. There generally is a bigger story, a more nuanced context, waiting for further information to reveal itself.

Much is lost in this rush towards a Newtonian fast food psychology. Indeed, physicists have gone beyond Newton to understand that the universe works in more nuanced ways. It comes down to a basic reality that some may find harsh: physicists do physics much better than psychologists. However, don't despair if you are a psychologist – if we stop trying to be physicists, we may do psychology pretty well.

References

Atwood M (1985/2017). *The Handmaid's Tale*. Toronto: Penguin Random House Canada.

Laing RD (1990). *The Politics of Experience and the Bird of Paradise*. London: Penguin Books.

Meehl PE (1954/2013). *Clinical Versus Statistical Prediction: a theoretical analysis and a review of the evidence*. Minneapolis, MN: University of Minnesota Press.

Newton I (1999). *The Principia: mathematical principles of natural philosophy* (Cohen IB, Whitman A, trans). Oakland, CA: University of California Press.

Rich A (1978). XIII. In: *The Dream of a Common Language: poems 1974-1977*. New York, NY: WW Norton & Co.

Tyson ND (2017). *Astrophysics for People in a Hurry*. New York, NY: WW Norton & Co.

3
Paradigms lost

I am not what you see and hear.
Hal Incandenza (Wallace, 1996)

I am not a physicist, but I am in love with the evolving and increasingly weird conceptualisations that spring from physicists' extraordinary minds. Reflecting on ideas and movements in psychology *vis à vis* some of the revolutionary developments in physics may remind us of the richness and power of neglected ways of being with and seeing other people in our haste to adopt a more Newtonian mindset. The world of each individual I come across is unique, complex beyond measure, and always changing. These inner worlds defy any attempt at Newtonian reduction, and we fool ourselves if we think we have succeeded when taking that path. The individual is lost, and I believe we also lose something of our own humanity in the process.

Reflecting on quantum physics and Einstein's theories appears to offer some escape from our Newtonian traps in psychology, as long as we are aware, in the end, that we are still not physicists. For me, an even better model for considering work with another person is one that is grounded in ethics, not science, and I will explore that soon enough. However, for the present exploration, I borrow some key concepts from post-Newtonian physics as starting points or useful frames for considering our work with people and, more importantly, with individuals. I will limit myself to four concepts that I find particularly relevant to psychology and valuing the individual.

The first concept, which for me is still the most astounding and mind boggling, is that the rules for how the world operates break down at the sub-atomic level: the world is not what it appears to be underneath it all. Another concept, perhaps not readily appreciated outside of physics, is the dual nature of light, or what is referred to as wave-particle duality. Rounding out my little amateur foray into post-Newtonian physics are Heisenberg's uncertainty principle and Einstein's theory of relativity.

Let's begin with weirdness. The world operates differently at the sub-atomic level. When the scale of things is small enough, the usual laws of physics don't apply. When scientists began to recognise this and break free from having to see everything through Newton's frame, immense discoveries rapidly began to emerge. Physicists such as Planck, Bohr, Heisenberg and Einstein are heroes to me for questioning the seemingly unquestionable. They questioned reality itself and what, for centuries, we thought we knew about it. It turns out that the way big things all around us seem to work is not the same as the way little things work – things too small for us to see with our eyes. The rules we take for granted in the larger world break down and are not useful at the sub-atomic level.

Even what we think is happening in the larger world is relative to our frame of reference. Our usual concept of cause and effect breaks down, with multiple causes and effects occurring in different orders and simultaneously. Things can even change without the passage of time; sudden changes in sub-atomic patterns or configurations, quantum leaps. Weirdness ensues. Basically, reality is not what we think it is. And that reality, that weirdness, reflects the importance and almost impossible immensity of individuality considered at the level of each person's mind. As Jung once observed:

> To find out what is truly individual in ourselves, profound
> reflection is needed; and suddenly we realize how uncommonly
> difficult the discovery of individuality is. (1977: 155)

The individual mind emerges from a complex interaction of a person's unique brain, the rest of the person's also unique body, and the outer world, all of which are changing over time – ever-changing contexts, continually unfolding in an extraordinary and infinite kaleidoscopic process. What is happening in an individual's brain is hidden inside our skull and is at a level too small for us to see directly. Within the typical person's brain there are approximately one hundred billion neurons and approximately a quadrillion (one thousand trillion) connections between them. Beyond this tremendous number are countless variations of the overall interplay and changing patterns as messages continually speed along these connections, whether we are asleep or awake. Given the absolute uniqueness of each person's context, each person's mind is literally a universe of its own.

Freud understood that a unique set of rules operates in the world of the mind, and so he pursued a new way of seeing people. He attempted to apply observations of himself and his patients to develop an understanding of these unique 'rules' of the mind. These observations led him to an analysis of the psyche, which he unsurprisingly dubbed psychoanalysis. This new science was a science of the mind, with its own rules, acknowledging that rules of other sciences may not apply accurately. Freud developed general principles for the inner workings of the mind. He also explored and developed ingenious ways to examine what we cannot see, since we are always a step removed from someone's inner world. These include such things as dream analysis, analysis of the words we use and mistakenly use and analysis of somatic expressions as means of accessing and exploring our inner world from the outside. The general principles of Freud's new science of the mind gave a useful frame or way to orient the clinician, but the focus was always on a careful exploration of the individual's inner world through listening to their words and watching their behaviours. Although Freud theorised general processes, he assumed the individual's inner world had developed its own conflicts, its own metaphors and its own meanings – its own unique patterns. He honoured the individual's mind, with all of its vast complexity.

Jung also developed an understanding of the universal, through his understanding of archetypes and images that appear across cultures, and explained how this played out in the individual's mind. The universal might be observable in some sense and provide a frame for understanding and exploring, but the expression of the universal in the context of the individual was paramount. Common universal elements find a unique unfolding in each individual mind. Given all of the potential complexity of an individual's world, it takes time even to begin seeing and making some sense of it. Beyond the time it takes to begin to understand the individual, these psychodynamic ways of approaching an individual's world can take a lifetime for a psychologist to study and still never master. However, we don't have to reach some fictional or ideal level of mastery to find these approaches meaningful. The path itself offers enough insight, learning and wonder.

Jung was informed about contemporary developments in physics. He was aware that causation does not have to be in one direction: A leading forward in time to B. In quantum mechanics, effects can come before causes, or they can co-occur. When we do not conceive of things going forward in time, but rather consider a pattern that is eternal – literally meaning outside of time – other possibilities emerge. Jung explored this concept in his book *Synchronicity* (1973), the title of which may be commonly known but the heady concepts within it perhaps less so. He struggled with some very difficult ideas and questioned the notion that anything is truly coincidental. He asserted that coincidence can be meaningful and that coincidences can be linked in a way that may be thought of as acausal – not proceeding forward from A to B but forming part of an overall pattern. This led to an awareness that analysing what appear to be coincidences might bring further meaning to an exploration of a person's experience. Change is not linear; entire patterns of experience in the human mind can shift suddenly, not unlike the quantum leaps that appear to occur at the sub-atomic level. Becoming aware of and understanding the pattern that emerges can lead to deep change.

Fritz Perls saw that, when it comes to our minds, the whole is reflected in all of the parts. In his innovative Gestalt therapy, he conceived a sort of unified field theory of the mind. Start anywhere and you will find a path to yourself, your conflicts and your solutions. Empty-chair and Gestalt dream interpretation are wonderfully alive techniques that reflect this. Talking to yourself as if speaking from a part of yourself or speaking directly to a part of yourself can bring insight and lead to change. Because the various actors and even objects in dreams all reflect the greater whole in some way, recreating and inhabiting dreams from these different perspectives during therapy can bring about a fuller awareness. Everything is connected. The patterns of our individual experiences as they have unfolded over time are indeed rich beyond imagining.

Our understanding of light can also bring insights into how we see individuals. Among other things, Newton was famous for optics, his study of light. He theorised that light is made up of particles. Unfortunately, subsequent experiments conducted by others appeared to contradict him, supporting the notion that light was wave-like in nature. However, this contradiction came from the manner in which the experiments were designed. The understanding of light as a wave phenomenon persisted until Einstein convincingly explained its particle nature. These two theories of light – wave and particle – are seemingly contradictory. So, who turned out to be right and who turned out to be wrong? Where is the truth? Does light consist of waves or particles? It turns out the answer is yes. Light has a dual nature; it is not 'either or', it is 'both and'. Whether we see it as waves or particles depends on how we measure it. We can also see the human mind differently depending on what we are using to observe and measure. Seeing this as a contradiction is not necessary.

Just like light, individuals are wonderful sets of contradictions. Or, as Walt Whitman (1983: 72) proclaimed: 'Do I contradict myself? Very well then, (I contradict myself. I am large, I contain multitudes.)' No one theory is adequate to explain our minds and predict our behaviours. Having started out at the beginning of things as star stuff scattered across the universe, we are truly creatures of light. How could any effort at reducing us through one concrete lens, such as cognitive behavioural therapy, possibly reveal all there is? Any lens we apply does not hold the only truth. The truth it clarifies is only a partial one. Whatever we use to observe will dictate how and what we see. Different qualities emerge when we use different modes of understanding. If you only focus on thoughts, feelings and behaviours, that is what you will see.

There are infinite ways to see individuals, and we have seen an explosion of theories influencing the ways in which we can see and interact with other people. Each has its own truth. Freud, Jung, Adler, Perls, Frankl, Erikson, Skinner, Rogers and Beck, among many others, all stumbled upon some truth about who and what we are. Research continues to show the efficacy of wildly disparate approaches to psychotherapy, each emerging from a different theory of how our minds work and how change can occur. Perhaps we can learn from our physicist friends, who are able to hold in their brilliant minds contradictory truths about light and be comfortable with the simple awareness that there is no one way, or best way, to see the human mind. Each way simply leads us down a different path and sheds light on a different aspect of an individual's world.

The Heisenberg uncertainty principle is perhaps even more unsettling than wave-particle duality. Simply put, observing something affects it. There is no such thing as a pure observation in which the observer does not play a role of influence. Our relationship to things changes them. And, as many of us know, our relationships to other people change them and us. What we do as psychologists happens in a relationship, whether we are involved in psychotherapy or assessment. We have an impact on the people we work with beyond what we are intending. And they have an impact on us. Our impact on each other is ongoing and the mutual effect is always in the room. However, taking the principle a step further, it also means we can never fully know the other person because who we are affects how we see them and what they in turn show of themselves to us. We can never see the other person free from this web of influences. A comfort with uncertainty and ambiguity and our ultimate lack of any real control becomes an essential attitude.

Freud's theory of transference and countertransference mirrors this fundamental understanding from quantum physics. It describes the relationship between the observer and the observed and the mutual effect they have on each other, as opposed to the direct linear impact in Newtonian physics and at the heart of behavioural and cognitive behavioural approaches. The observer affects the observed (transference) and the observed affects the observer (countertransference). Also, our attempts to change people change us. Freud's observations were unflinching. He spent time with his patients. He got to know them as individuals. He also continually analysed himself and his reactions and how these could get in the way of being able to understand his patients. Because of his willingness to analyse himself and to listen beyond fear and disgust to his patients, he was able to develop a valuable model.

New research in neuroscience, such as Lisa Feldman Barrett's work (2017), seems to me to be consistent with Freud's concepts of transference and countertransference, developed about 100 years earlier. Our minds literally create what we see and experience. We enter into a relationship in which both of us are continually creating what we see and experience against the background of our contexts that we bring to the encounter. The psychoanalyst does his or her best to know themselves well enough to try to see more clearly beyond their own context and reactions in order to help their patient learn to see beyond theirs. Of course, this takes a great deal of effort on our part outside of the clinical relationship. Psychoanalysts work on themselves so as not to get stuck in the contexts they bring into the therapy relationship. The potential exists for getting lost in our own context and not seeing the other person, whether one practises from a psychodynamic frame or not.

Most people are aware of these concepts, leading to the inevitable conclusion that self-reflection and efforts at personal growth should be an essential part of the work that therapists do outside of therapy. I would add that it is also essential for those of us who engage in assessment work. For any number of reasons, this way of thinking seems no longer part of mainstream discourse in our field. Fewer psychologists appear to enter into psychotherapy for their own growth, which is perhaps another fast food casualty of our Newton-centric field. We come to mirror the mass production we engage in.

When the people we face in our work experience us and interact with us, it only makes sense that they will have reactions to us, and that those reactions will be shaped by the contexts built from an entire life history that they bring to each moment they are with us. This will influence how they experience us further and what they hear in what we say. At the same time, we also bring contexts built from our entire life history, through which we experience the person we are interacting with. In non-directive, person-centred approaches, we are unlikely to take conscious action to change other people based on this awareness. Nonetheless, we retain an awareness of the importance of knowing and accepting ourselves. We know that this affects the nature and quality of our interaction with other people. Like our psychodynamic friends, we may spend a good deal of time trying to understand our own processes better in an effort to avoid them interfering with fully hearing the people we work with.

Freud focused on knowing ourselves well enough so we don't get in the way of seeing the other person. Rogers described the importance of congruence (being comfortable in our own skin) and unconditional positive regard (an ability to hear the other person without judging them through the influence of our own potential discomforts) in the service of more readily and empathically understanding the other person. Rogers understood that attempting to empathically understand other people with a reasonable degree of accuracy requires us to understand ourselves. From this perspective, being able to work through and get past our judgements is part of our own personal work as clinicians. This is hard, messy and painful work at times. It is much simpler, and perhaps more comfortable, to ignore it, focus on categorising thoughts, feelings and behaviours and come up with practical solutions after operationalising the problems that people share with us.

Rogers has been reduced by some to being a Skinnerian thinker. Essentially, this reductionist understanding holds that we create conditions as therapists to reinforce a natural tendency in people to grow positively. If we respond in a certain way to people, this will have the desired effect of bringing about change in them. In other words, we can behaviourally reinforce what Rogers described as the actualising tendency. However, what this way of thinking misses is that Rogers came to the conclusion that positive change, transformative growth, happens in relationship, and in particular a certain kind of relationship that the person we work with experiences. It is an essentially interactional theory. It is I-Thou (Buber, 1970), in an ongoing interplay, not action A causing effect B; me changing you.

I believe that seeing the actualising tendency concept as Skinnerian is a significant reductionist mistake. Rogers posited that this tendency towards growth exists in all of us, and in all forms of life. However, when it comes to human growth, it is fostered under certain conditions, and these conditions are clearly relational. That is why I have elsewhere described the actualising tendency as a myth (Levitt, 2008), a useful guiding story within the relationship. It is a theory, a touchstone of sorts, that may allow us to more openly see and value human nature in all of its countless and ever-changing expressions. In this manner, it may serve to help us stay connected and engaged in a relationship at those times when it is most difficult to do so, rather than running in fear or disgust, or shutting down from boredom. It is at the core of a relational theory.

The challenge of observing other people ultimately lies in our complete inability to experience another person's experience, no matter how much we may fool ourselves to the contrary. It is also one of the conclusions we must reach when we think about observing other people in light of the Heisenberg uncertainty principle. No approach can ever grant us direct access to another person's experiences. This is where Einstein's theory of relativity may be relevant. There may be absolutes, but some things are also relative. Frames of reference matter. An individual's experience is a unique frame of reference. An individual's context holds its own value as a source of meaning and depth. All things in an individual's inner world become relevant in their own way and only really make sense when they are not crammed into our own boxes and measured from inside our own frames, our own ways of seeing the world. Freud understood this when he highlighted the importance of therapists dealing with their own countertransference (their issues) when attempting to observe and understand another person's frame as fully and cleanly as possible. Yet, as RD Laing (1990: 15) rightly observed with a poetic perfection uniquely his own, that 'frame', that actual experience of the other person, will always be out of reach to us: 'I see you, and you see me. I experience you, and you experience me. I see your behaviour. You see my behaviour. But I do not and never will see your *experience* of me.'

The idea that what is real depends on the frame of reference is a powerful one. It is a reminder that none of us is able to hold the ultimate truth about another person; we are only able to experience them from inside our own frame of reference. The danger when we assume there is some universal or Newtonian frame is that we may think we know what it is and push that frame on others, stubbornly insisting we have understood them. Our science can become our unwitting ally in this regard. This is the failure of not recognising the importance of the subjective, the frame of the other person, whether in therapy or assessment contexts. When we acknowledge the reality and importance of the other person's frame as distinct from our own, or as distinct from an external frame represented by numbers, we are recognising and valuing the subjective.

Milton Erickson had an unusual facility for working as if he could enter another person's frame. He was a genius in this regard, describing people as living in their own unique trance states. He would fashion a hypnotic suggestion of sorts that was tailored specifically to enter and find acceptance in the unique world of the other person, attempting to shift their world from within their own trance state. Art Bohart (2008) also captured with great beauty this awareness of the unique frame of the individual's own reality in his chapter, 'How Clients Self-Heal in Psychotherapy', in my book, *Reflections on Human Potential* (Levitt, 2008). He observed that what people find effective in therapy is often not what we think it is and may even be what we thought was a failure on our part. This is very humbling for all of us who hold fast to our theories and apply techniques honed by years of training and experience and backed by solid research. What each of us may think of as reality is relative; the other person's frame of reference really does matter and has great value.

For Rogers, a values-based approach recognises the frame of the other people as valuable in its own right. He argues against imposing our own frame on other people. Rather, for Rogers, the goal is to understand the person as if from their frame, not our own. He further understood the importance of the other person experiencing our attempt to understand them without judgement. This can only occur when we, as therapists, are comfortable enough not to feel the need to impose our own frame. Recognising the wisdom and power of another person's frame and making the choice to honour it rather than impose our own is a political and ethical stance. It requires leaving the comfort of our frame. It requires recognising the illusion that our frame is somehow universal or absolute and readily applied to others. It also requires a comfort in ourselves so we can be with a person in their experience without feeling so threatened as to need to change it, shut it up or make it us, which is just another way of changing it or shutting it up. To reach this comfort requires a certain degree of awareness of what makes us uncomfortable and coming to terms with it so we don't have to change it to our own frame. It requires humility.

Embracing complexity and uncertainty is not easy to package, sell and teach. Nor is the notion of giving up control. Yet all of this leads to more nuanced understandings of the other person as more than an imposed set of categories to be acted on. Other people are more than thoughts, feelings and behaviours to be changed. There are manifold variables that cloud our view of the other person's frame, aside from the futility of ever being able to see it fully. A unique life with its own complexity, agency and worth is easily lost in the prevailing Newtonian frame. Under this reductionist paradigm we have also lost the wonder of coincidence, the richness of metaphor, the poetry of dreams and the aliveness and immediacy of the encounter. We have lost the uniqueness of the other person.

Clinicians such as Freud, Jung, Laing, Rogers and Perls all described a willingness to engage in discomfort, messiness, oddness, boredom, fear and discomfort – a willingness to push past alienation;

a willingness to face the uniqueness of the other person in her or his fullness. Although it may seem otherwise, given the dominance of cognitive behavioural approaches in our field, these paradigms have never really been lost. As guiding stories and sources of wonder and inspiration, the ideas in these paradigms remain powerful and ready to take on new life at any time. All we have to do is seek them out. Science does not have to be dead.

References

Barrett LF (2017). *How Emotions are Made: the secret life of the brain*. Boston, MA: Mariner Books.

Bohart A (2008). How clients self-heal in psychotherapy. In: Levitt BE (ed). *Reflections on Human Potential: bridging the person-centred approach and positive psychology*. Ross-on-Wye: PCCS Books (pp175–186).

Buber M (1970). *I and Thou* (W Kaufmann, trans). New York, NY: Touchstone.

Jung CG (1977). *Two Essays on Analytical Psychology* (2nd ed revised and augmented) (RFC Hull, trans). Princeton, NJ: Princeton University Press.

Jung CG (1973). *Synchronicity*. Princeton, NJ: Princeton University Press.

Laing RD (1990). *The Politics of Experience and the Bird of Paradise*. London: Penguin Books.

Levitt BE (ed) (2008). *Reflections on Human Potential: bridging the person-centred approach and positive psychology*. Ross-on-Wye: PCCS Books.

Wallace DF (1996). *Infinite Jest*. New York, NY: Little, Brown and Co.

Whitman W (1983). 'Song of myself'. In: Whitman W. *Leaves of Grass*. New York, NY: Bantam Books.

Part 2

Beyond theory
and control

4

The cult of personality theory

First you learn the instrument, then you learn the music, then you forget all that shit and just play.
Charlie Parker (numerous sources and varied versions)

Museums are monuments to our need for classification and control. I will never forget my first visit to the British Museum in London. It houses an entire Greek temple, with a rich spiritual past literally torn from its foundations and put on display. There's a room full of Egyptians, mummified and in their sarcophagi, no longer at rest beneath Egyptian soil – butterflies pinned under glass. From one room to the next, this extraordinary display of power, conquest and domination unfolds. It is breathtaking and horrific at the same time.

I had just finished a university course on Roman civilisation, and my term project was a survey of Roman portrait sculpture. I had reviewed hundreds upon hundreds of years of changing styles that reflected other cultures subjugated through this mighty empire's terrible wars of conquest and made Roman by its artisans. And now I was in the British Museum, discovering in its many rooms the very portrait sculptures I had studied, from the small to the colossal – the history of a once-powerful empire brought under the magnifying glass of another. In room after room I saw culture after culture brought under control and placed on display, neatly categorised and chronicled. I was young and even then it made my feet sore and my mind dizzy as I walked through this vast storehouse. Here was a cold statement of overwhelming power. To classify is to control, and to control is to exercise power.

Classification as a means of exercising power over others has ancient roots:

> And the Lord God fashioned from the soil each beast of the field and each fowl of the heavens and brought each to the human to see what he would call it, and whatever the human called a living creature, that was its name. (Alter, 2004: 22)

Naming holds the power to shape reality. The one who names is the one who holds power in a relationship; in ancient terms, they 'hold dominion' over others. Naming remains a common practice today and, as a system of classification, is used by science as a way to organise things in groups, to categorise them, so we can try to understand them better. It is, of course, a useful exercise in many ways and can help us develop our knowledge. When I was 10 years old, I learned how to categorise rocks. I still remember how much fun it was, collecting them and figuring out their classifications. I soon learned many things can be classified in order to study them: plants, animals and elements can all be grouped in a classification scheme, to be observed and studied with scientific methods. It was exciting.

The problem when we classify and categorise even something like a rock is that we can easily lose our sense of wonder in the moment. We can lose our more direct awareness of what is essential and unique about the rock we pick up from the grass that catches our eye during a stroll. Even having a word for it, a name, removes us from the more immediate experience. What is essential is hidden in plain sight behind a name and category. The quality of our connections is changed by classifying. But we gain some sense of comfort knowing that we have a name for it, a group for it and a way of feeling we understand it better. It is more solidly under our control. And the more we classify, the more we gain expertise in our classification system, which tends to be a pretty satisfying experience. Also, the classifiers go unexamined in the process. It's a cosy arrangement.

While it can be useful, classification also can be a dubious and dangerous enterprise. Phrenology held a certain attraction during its brief period of popularity in the 19th century. Of course, we know we cannot determine a person's character, personality or the nature of their distress simply by examining the shape of their head. Nonetheless, classifying is a part of our social and scientific order, a part of how we go about learning things, and phrenology is a curious reminder of this human proclivity. Racial theory is perhaps one of the most dangerous manifestations of our compulsion to classify. Any reasonable person can see readily that racial theory is racist. Racial theory is dressed up as science through a manipulation of classification to justify the atrocities of empire and the position and privileges of those who hold power. And it is all about power – a dominant group studying the other and justifying itself.

Racial classifications remain, and where there is race there is racism. Caucasoid, Mongoloid, Negroid – these are meaningless terms scientifically. Socially, they hold great power. Their use implies a racist hierarchy. We don't often think of the latter two terms when we use the commonly accepted and seemingly acceptable term 'Caucasian', but they are hiding close by, in plain sight. Their existence as a part of a hierarchy is implied. Even diagnosis, a classification system backed by abundant research studies that follow the scientific method, has dangers that are hidden in plain sight. As it is with all classification systems, the one who diagnoses remains safe from the same scrutiny and objectification.

Then there are personality theories, which stand alongside diagnosis as essential classification systems in our field. Like diagnoses, they serve as a means to classify others, to understand and predict others in order to manipulate, change and control them. These theories are compasses that can orient us. In other words, they lead us in a particular direction, eliminating alternative paths and restricting an otherwise broader view. During my master's studies, we were encouraged to figure out which theoretical orientation to psychotherapy fit us best, which compass we wanted to use. We were schooled in various ideas from what we might now call the Golden Age of personality theories: Freud, Jung, Adler, Perls, Frankl, Rogers, Skinner, Beck.

Rogerian theory is a sort of anti-theory of personality, in contrast to other approaches. It does not provide a theory of personalities as a framework to think about and understand people. It also does not provide a foundation for techniques to change people. Rather, it offers a set of values-based attitudes for interacting with people as individuals with their own realities, without attempting to fit them into theoretical boxes. Client-centred theory is a guide for the development of clinician attitudes that can help us to approach and value people's experiences or 'theories' of themselves. In a reversal of the scientific classification approach, client-centred practitioners don't name other people; rather, we are open to knowing how they name themselves and what this means to them.

Nonetheless, client-centred theory is an orientation to clinical work and opens us to some of the inevitable vulnerabilities of other therapeutic orientations that come from identifying with them. During my master's studies, my classmates and I began to identify with different approaches: I am psychodynamic, I am cognitive behavioural, I am existential, I am client-centred. We did our best to recognise where we might fit in this world of theories about people that were developed by a handful of other people. The names of the progenitors of these theories continue to carry a certain power, and their personalities remain alive in some sense through our identification with their theories.

We are usually exposed to personality theories in an introductory course. We then pursue further learning in specific orientations through specialised coursework and training with supervisors who identify with the orientation we are interested in developing. When we are just starting out in the field, we are faced with a number of significant pressures: the enormity of all that we have to learn, the suffering of people who come to us for help, and the clear reality of our lack of experience. It is only natural, in the face of these pressures, to turn to ready-made theories and more knowledgeable supervisors to find the answers we need. Theories and techniques give us answers now. We feel compelled to seek out something that seems of value to offer people who are suffering when they are sitting in front of us. This is further compounded by our experience of being inexperienced, and perhaps the fear of being seen as a fraud or incompetent when we first start assessing and treating people. My guess is that many clinicians with years of experience still see themselves, at least at times, as frauds, despite their actual talent.

Not only is it difficult to experience the pressure of people suffering and seeking help from us; it is also hard for supervisors to face the pressure of young clinicians coming to us for the answers, a bag of tricks. It is easier to teach theories and techniques and to create manuals than to teach a way of questioning and exploring values within the context of assessment and treatment relationships. It is not surprising that even Rogers' client-centred therapy has been adapted by some as a set of techniques. It takes time to develop an understanding and lived experience of values as they play out in our work. It also takes time to develop a nuanced appreciation for theory and technique and, hopefully, to be able to reflect on them without being controlled by them. But at least with technique there are obvious, basic starting points that are easier to teach, easier to learn and easier to bring into the work we do with people who are suffering.

At the beginning of our journey of insecurity, we enter the field and are encouraged to adopt another person's way of thinking, before ever really gaining experience and finding our own way of thinking and connecting with others. We then gain further and further experience through adopting another person's mindset or theory, perhaps taking us further from ourselves. Before long, our identity as a clinician hardens in the mould of a theoretical orientation into which we have chosen to pour ourselves. And this is where many of us remain. It is likely to be very difficult for us, after so many years of coursework and applying what we have learned, to let it all go, especially if that has become our identity and an important source of comfort and self-esteem.

Considering our work beyond theory and control can be threatening. Our early development as clinicians involves taking course after course to learn theories, techniques and diagnostic formulations. We earn a degree that validates our achievement in filling our heads with an enormous amount of specialised information. We then bring this learning into our work. Through experience over time, we gain expertise and, perhaps, a certain standing with our colleagues and a degree of their respect. The power of a degree and expertise can be a frightening thing, especially when it gives us entry into working with other people who are vulnerable in some way. I believe it is an important stage of professional growth to move beyond theories and categories as things that we think are real. Unfortunately, the pull of these ways of thinking is powerful and subtle. We may not be able to see beyond them once we have achieved a certain level of expertise. It may mean giving up too much. Too much of our identity is already given over to the cult of our theoretical orientation.

The theories we turn to are an extraordinary reflection of those who created them and the contexts in which they lived. Their brilliance and unique ways of orienting to other people in their work are expressed through their theories, which also carry with them the strength of their personalities that continues to exert influence on others. Each found their own way to approach their work with other people. Freud's psychoanalysis was Freud's solution. Jung's psychoanalysis was Jung's solution. Client-centred therapy was Rogers' solution.

Without embarking on an exhaustive exploration, it is clear that much of Freud's thinking stems from his Jewish roots. But he was also a Jew living in Vienna; he was very aware of the polite veneer of his society; he was also most assuredly aware of the anti-semitism around him, despite that politeness and the degree of acceptance he had gained. He also witnessed how the veneer was quickly torn away in two savage wars, revealing an ugliness in people that was always just beneath the surface. His theory of personality is understandable in this context, with its themes of conflict, brutality, and the powerful importance of what goes unseen and unacknowledged. Jung's explorations derive from his very personal quest to understand his own severe distress, his own 'madness', documented in painstaking detail in his *Red Book* (2009). As with Freud, much of Jung's thinking stems from in-depth personal exploration as a starting point for trying to understand others. And, again as with Freud, it was his own starting point, unique to him and his personal life context.

Frankl's logotherapy (2006), his awareness of the importance of making meaning in life, emerged from the horrors of the concentration camps of Nazi Germany. Rogers' client-centred theory bears the hallmarks of American individualism, along with the influence of his Christian upbringing. Cognitive behavioural theories reflect the computer age, the rise of mass production and fast food culture and the ascendance of science and technology as the solution to all our modern problems. The individual personality as such no longer matters. All that matters are thoughts, feelings and behaviours as categories that we can recognise and change to solve people's 'problems in living'. We can even give people a user manual and teach them to be their own mechanics. These mechanical approaches are, in a sense, personality theories without personalities, regardless of the social skills and caring of the clinicians who adopt them.

Each personality theory in the panoply of theories that now exists holds a kind of particularist truth, but not a single one from this multitude is Truth. Each has its own allure, its own call, perhaps a siren song that draws us in without us realising our identities are being dashed against the rocks. Without a strong sense of self, we can give ourselves over to the cult of our choosing and find security there. We are at our most vulnerable in this regard when we first enter the field. And we over-identify with a theory as if it were real. Jung was not comfortable with the idea of Jungian followers. When a colleague of mine told Rogers that she was a Rogerian, he also reacted with discomfort. I believe both men realised that their ideas could take on a cult status, and they recognised that this was problematic.

I read a wonderful book on psychotherapy by Sheldon Kopp almost 30 years ago and the title, which carries this same theme, remains with me: *If You Meet the Buddha on the Road, Kill Him!* Kopp wrote:

> Killing the Buddha on the road means destroying the hope that anything outside of ourselves can be our master. No one is any bigger than anyone else. There are no mothers or fathers for grown-ups, only sisters and brothers. (1976: 188)

In other words, if we want to grow up as clinicians, we have to find a way to leave our cults, and this is what personality theories ultimately are. When you join a cult of personality theory, a cult to classify, not only are you removed from other people, you are also removed from yourself. You give away your authority and your experience. Considering this, why would we follow someone else's personality theory of other people without question, confining ourselves by identifying with it completely in order to understand other people we encounter?

There is a huge and wondrous world beyond theory and control, and it lives in infinite variety in the experiences of all the people we encounter. However, in order to let go of theory and control, it may be necessary to trust that there is actually something else that will fill the void, something we can move towards in a post-theoretical way of being. A first step can be growing our awareness that our theoretical concepts are not real. In saying this, I do not mean that theoretical concepts are not potentially useful or helpful. But theories are not real. It is a mistake to confuse a theory with actual people and the experiences of the individuals we encounter. Also, when we believe theoretical constructs are real and over-identify with them, we lose ourselves to what we have learned. We alienate ourselves from other people and ourselves. At the same time, it is hard work learning to synthesise all the ideas we are taught without getting stuck in them and slipping into a mindset of believing in them.

I am not suggesting that theories are bad or that it is wrong to study them. I am also not suggesting that the techniques that flow from these theories are bad and should not be used. I understand that there is ample research supporting the use of certain techniques in certain situations. However, I would suggest it is important when we are trying to work with other people to treat theories as guiding stories that we can let go of readily, not as realities. It is essential that we find a way to be more fully with another person's suffering without feeling compelled to rush in with a technique. Theories are rich and hold great potential as invitations to further thought and self-reflection. Rather than abandoning them, I am suggesting that we learn to have a healthier relationship to them.

The obvious question to ask ourselves is what are we to do if we look towards an approach that is not guided by a theory of other people or founded on techniques? Client-centred practitioners are often already there, especially those who started their training with a foundation in this values-based approach. This does not mean they are free from the lure of cult identity, the power of cult mind, but they do tend not to feel the need to place other people into theories, to categorise, name and diagnose them. Carl Rogers' radical suggestion was to start with the person facing him and attempt to understand that person as fully as possible from their own perspective. He recognised that this act required understanding the values we hold when we face people. He focused on understanding our way of being with other people, rather than holding tightly to theories about them.

Although Rogers' work was grounded in science, ethics remained an essential perspective. He emphasised the value of the other person, rather than the value of theory and techniques. Instead of abandoning our science, perhaps we can develop a deeper appreciation for the way ethics brings science to life through a return to the encounter. A values-driven approach can offer a solid foundation that allows for exquisite flexibility in our attempts to understand people.

As with personality theories, there are myriad sources of learning and ways of developing values to carry into our relationships with other people. Many of these sources are outside psychology and have been around a very, very long time. Art, poetry, literature, music, philosophy, science and religion are all potential sources we can turn to in order to explore values as the foundation for our interactions with other people. These apparently disparate fields have some common strands woven through them that lead to an understanding that everything is connected. The source and substance of all things as they continually unfold is one. Everything is star stuff. This is stated elegantly in the Shema, the central call of prayer in Judaism. It finds development in such ethical statements as Hillel's famous summation of *Torah*: 'What you find abhorrent to yourself, do not do to your neighbour.'

Reflecting on this notion of connectedness may provide a starting point for considering our relation to other people. However, we may struggle to accept this basic concept when a mystic or a spiritual leader says it, or when we see it quoted from the Bible or another spiritual source. This is especially true in today's secular world. We may have an almost reflexive discomfort when we hear this idea from these sources. It may be easier to recognise our great artists telling us this through their masterpieces. Van Gogh thought he was a failed minister, but his masterpieces are powerful sermons conveying the interconnectedness of all things. Whitman saw worth and dignity in all people and things, no matter how small or low, and found a way to express this with his uninhibited and loving poet's voice, in poems he often called songs. For Whitman, even a pea could be worthy of our full attention and respect, or as he put it: 'There is no object so soft but it makes a hub for the wheeled universe' (1983: 70). Bach's ability to bring different voices together, unfolding together as one over time while still remaining distinct, reached its greatest expression in his fugues. Einstein elegantly stated that energy and matter are the same thing: $E = mc^2$. He also described the oneness of the space-time fabric. Physicists continue in their quest for a unified field theory, a theory of everything, that relates the concepts of Newtonian and quantum physics.

The humanistic shift toward valuing the individual finds its fullest expression in Carl Rogers' work, which breaks free from describing individuals and their experiences in theoretical terms. Instead he explored the factors that promote positive change and growth within the context of a relationship. The development of his ethical thinking is largely grounded, as one would imagine, in a Christian sensibility. Do unto others. Love the stranger. Turn the other cheek. Judge not. Take the log out of your own eye. Yet Rogers did not develop a theory in Christian terms rationalised by Christ's teachings. He turned to science. He found support from research into the factors that actually promote growth and positive change in what he described as a transformative relationship. This research formed the basis for his non-directive approach, and he laid out its foundations in six basic principles (1959: 213), stated simply as:

1. That two persons are in contact.

2. That the first person, whom we shall term the client, is in a state of incongruence, being vulnerable, or anxious.

3. That the second person, whom we shall term the therapist, is congruent in the relationship.

4. That the therapist is experiencing unconditional positive regard toward the client.

5. That the therapist is experiencing an empathic understanding of the client's internal frame of reference.

6. That the client perceives, at least to a minimal degree, conditions 4 and 5, the unconditional positive regard of the therapist for him, and the empathic understanding of the therapist.

Rogers offered his scientifically grounded framework about 60 years ago, and it still holds within it great potential for developing values for approaching our clinical work with other people. When he called his approach non-directive, he meant this as a statement about developing our awareness of the way power is expressed in relationships in order to learn how to value the other person more fully; he did not intend it as a directive to be passive and just repeat back to people things that they tell us. In my first book (Levitt, 2005), I gathered together people I saw as thought leaders in the person-centred world to flesh out what it means to be non-directive. Each expressed their own, unique understanding and experience of this concept, and the curious reader interested in exploring multiple perspectives may wish to read what they say. For me it is as simple and as challenging as letting go of the need for holding power over the other person. Everything springs from that one idea, which I have described as a foundational attitude (Levitt, 2005).

To let go of power over another is to let go of the need to define them and judge them, the need to categorise and classify them. This requires us to feel safe and comfortable in our own being in order to be with another person and not be threatened by the reality they share with us. To love the stranger, we have to recognise also how we are strangers and love our own strangeness. Rogers was getting at this with his second and third principles. In order to enter into a transformative relationship with someone in distress, we have to know our own shit and be comfortable in our skin. This does not mean we have to be perfectly actualised beings. That is, of course, impossible. Rather, it means we have to know ourselves well enough to recognise when we are being triggered in ways that stop us from being fully present to another person's experience. We have to be brave enough and value the other person enough to do something when we are aware that this is happening in the moment. This is an ongoing effort on the part of the clinician who recognises that their own discomforts are the greatest barrier to seeing other people and valuing them for who they are. These discomforts can hide safely in the way we hold onto our theories and techniques and our professional roles, in the way we structure our work, and in the other very clever places that we fool ourselves into thinking are real and necessary.

For me, to value other people means being able to recognise first that they are indeed other people, with their own unique and full experience and the right to make choices and direct their own lives. This means recognising and letting go of the ways I might exercise control or power over them. They have a right to exercise their own power without my interference. In order for me to see another person as more than just an other, I have to be aware of and push beyond my judgements and reactions that get in the way of being able to appreciate them. This doesn't mean that I have to agree with them or see things the same way as them. It does mean that I don't need them to agree with me and see things the same way I see them. This stance is a basic embrace of the other person's unique value; it is a stance of humility that acknowledges I am not more valuable than the person I am encountering and that they, too, have a full and alive experience that flows from their own life context and being.

Understanding a person through a theoretical formulation is necessarily an act of objectification. It distances us, creating a barrier to seeing the other person more fully. When we say we value other people and then objectify them, I believe we are lying to ourselves about who we are actually valuing. If I value another individual for who they are, in their own fullness, it makes sense to me that I would try to understand them on their own terms, in their own language, from their own point of view. Whatever I do to get in the way of this devalues them, because I am valuing my own understanding and myself more.

Valuing other people, for me, means not confining them to maps of my own or someone else's making. I trust people to be their own living maps that they may still be unfolding and charting, discovering and redrafting. This is how I have come to understand Rogers' fourth and fifth principles; holding unconditional positive regard for other people and attempting to empathically understand them from their frame and not my own are one and the same. Attempting to listen in a theory-free way, free of judgements, requires me to be comfortable in myself, which Rogers might describe as a state of congruence. These principles, as I experience them, flow into each other and hold together as a sort of oneness. Distinguishing these as different and separately definable principles is artificial and comes from a need to find a way to express them in writing, taking the form of theory. It reifies them unnecessarily.

I don't think it is possible to fully listen empathically without also fully prizing the other person. I also don't think it is possible to fully prize the other person without making an effort to fully understand them empathically. And, if we don't know ourselves and are not comfortable with ourselves, this will necessarily limit our ability to prize and hear other people. Ultimately, when we embody these types of values, people tend to see or feel it, and hopefully then trust us enough to reveal themselves to us while facing themselves. People know when we are judging them. People also know when they have not been seen or understood. The more the people we work with experience judgement and not being understood, the less likely we are to be actually seeing them.

Before moving on from Rogers' principles, it is worth taking some time to consider the first principle: 'That two persons are in contact.' This seems so obvious that it was generally taken for granted, and perhaps even ignored. That is, until a gentle genius named Garry Prouty came along. I always remember his hearty, infectious laugh and his bear hugs that lifted me off my feet. Garry was very human and humble, and he worked with people many of us ignore or are afraid of: people diagnosed with schizophrenia and profound developmental disabilities. Since the Wisconsin Project (Rogers, 1967), which researched the effectiveness of the client-centred approach with people diagnosed with schizophrenia, it was assumed that the approach simply was not effective. Garry found otherwise; he was able to successfully connect with people others struggled to connect with, and his mentor, Gene Gendlin, suggested that he describe what he was doing (Prouty, 1994).

Garry did not see his approach as a technique, although it was perhaps simplest to break it down and teach it that way. But breaking it down into theory changes it. When we try to put down on paper what we are doing, we lose the aliveness of it. It becomes reified in words, and we are left with a pale imitation, a shrine in print to which we pay homage. The theory distances us from what actually happens in the moment, in that perhaps undefinable place that exists in a relationship. The human element, when put down into words to describe what we are doing, can quickly become a thing, and the relational elements can easily flatten into a technique. Having watched Garry work and having been lucky enough to chat with him regularly, that is not where the magic is.

What I experienced through knowing Garry and watching him was a lesson in consciousness-raising and seeing the other person more fully. He once told me that working with people who were not yet in contact with themselves, the world or us required being comfortable with watching paint dry. Garry was attuned to the slower and more subtle processes in the worlds of other people who many of us feel unable to 'reach'. To be in contact with people who are hard to be in contact with requires a certain kind of valuing and empathic awareness, and this is what Garry found, without having to hold power over them. His work with people who many of us would find too challenging to work with was a powerful reminder that it is really about being able to get past our own shit to appreciate the other person, no matter how strange or alien they seem. We have to get past our over-identification with a theory. We have to break free from cults of personality theory. If I had to say it succinctly, as a reminder to myself, I would say, 'It's about the other person, stupid.'

As I alluded to earlier, even the person-centred approach is vulnerable to taking on a cult status for those who practise it. Even with the person-centred approach, we can come to believe that our theoretical constructs and concepts are real things. I began to question this when I described the actualising tendency concept as a myth (Levitt, 2008). We may hold to a rigid understanding of how we should respond in order to be good practitioners of any theoretical orientation we adhere to. Within the person-centred world, we may judge ourselves or others for not carrying the values of the approach into the rest of our daily lives and interactions. We may judge ourselves or others for not engaging in empathic understanding correctly, which is one of the reasons I dislike research that reifies this concept. It moves away from recognising that empathic understanding flows as a by-product of valuing the other person's unique world as distinct from our own. We may find ourselves sitting in judgement over other approaches and missing out on the richness they have to offer because we are lost to our own cult.

After finishing my second book (Levitt, 2008), I remember feeling that I had contributed what I needed to about non-directivity; that, through collaboration with amazing people from around the world, my books addressed a certain gap in the literature that I was surprised existed and that I felt needed to be filled. I felt a real sense of closure that gave me the strength to move on and take on a nomadic life outside of the person-centred world. I consciously set out on a personal journey away from the person-centred world, perhaps vaguely recognising that I needed to be more aware of my attachments to and identification with the theory. I left listserves and community events, but I retained friendships with person-centred colleagues who will always be dear to me. Sadly, during that decade, I also lost both of my non-directive parents, Barbara Brodley and Garry Prouty. I became not only a nomad but also an orphan, and I found new family, new colleagues, none of whom were connected to the person-centred community. I made my home with them, learning from their different perspectives and relearning who I am as a clinician simply by doing the work, day after day. I have grown to love my nomadic life, better appreciating the clinicians around me with their differing perspectives and unique gifts. I have also come to better appreciate my own perspective and way of being, and to love deeply what I do. Every day I strive to work beyond theory and control, free myself from cults of personality theory, let go of all that shit, and just play.

References

Alter R (2004). *The Five Books of Moses: a translation with commentary*. New York, NY: WW Norton & Co.

Frankl VE (2006). *Man's Search for Meaning*. Boston, MA: Beacon Press.

Jung CG (2009). *The Red Book: liber novus* (S Shamdassani, ed). New York, NY: WW Norton & Company.

Kopp SB (1976). *If You Meet the Buddha on the Road, Kill Him! The pilgrimage of psychotherapy patients*. Toronto: Bantam Books.

Levitt BE (ed) (2008). *Reflections on Human Potential: bridging the person-centred approach and positive psychology*. Ross-on-Wye: PCCS Books.

Levitt BE (ed) (2005). *Embracing Non-Directivity: reassessing person-centred theory and practice in the 21st century*. Ross-on-Wye: PCCS Books.

Prouty G (1994). *Theoretical Evolutions in Person-Centered Therapy: applications to schizophrenics and retarded psychoses*. Westport, CT: Prager.

Rogers CR (ed) (1967). *The Therapeutic Relationship and its Impact: a study with schizophrenics*. Madison, WI: University of Wisconsin Press.

Rogers CR (1959). A theory of therapy, personality and interpersonal relationships as developed in the client-centred framework. In: Koch S (ed). *Psychology: a study of a science*. New York, NY: McGraw-Hill (pp184–216).

Whitman W (1983). Song of myself. In: Whitman W. *Leaves of Grass*. New York, NY: Bantam Books (p70).

5

Diagnosis disorder

And as an individual perceives the extent of dehumanization, he or she may ask if humanization is a viable possibility.
Paolo Freire (1994: 25)

People often ask me if they are crazy. It is essential that we hear this question in the moment, with all of the nuanced meanings it may carry for the person asking it. It is often an expression of vulnerability. Many of the people I encounter in my work are afraid they might be crazy, whatever this may mean to them. That fear is powerfully isolating and alienating. The stigma of craziness is a heavy weight to carry when you think the word 'crazy' applies to you. The personal meanings this carries for each person that make it so heavy for them only add to their isolation. It is a lot to unpack and share, but three words strung together in the form of a question 'Am I crazy?' are a courageous call to us from deep within another person. So much pain and distress are wrapped up in this question. It is all the more brave when someone asks it of a person who carries the socially and legally sanctioned authority to diagnose it. Asking another person, 'Am I crazy?' also makes facing it all the more real. Have I become 'that'? Am I irretrievably lost, irreparably broken? Is there any hope for me? Am I dirty? Am I bad? Am I alone? Am I no longer human? Am I sick in the head?

Sick in the head. This may be the most common understanding we have of people experiencing emotional distress. And sometimes it is true. There are actual brain diseases and chemical imbalances that are entirely consistent with the medical model. It is useful and important to know the difference between dementia and delirium and to know the signs of a stroke. A differential diagnosis can help determine if a medication will be helpful or harmful. Diagnosing these conditions can dramatically impact people's lives for the better.

Unfortunately, the medical model can be over-extended, particularly when emotional distress is seen as an illness. For the interested reader who has not considered this, Thomas Szasz's seminal *The Myth of Mental Illness* (2010) is an excellent starting point. Each new edition of the *Diagnostic and Statistical Manual of Mental Disorders* (*DSM*) makes it easier to see the medicalisation of distress. The current edition, *DSM-5* (American Psychiatric Association, 2013), dwarfs the first, which was published back in 1952. It now includes diagnoses for such fundamental experiences of human distress as grief. It is not unreasonable to consider the possibility that anything that can be masked or enhanced with medication may become a diagnostic category in future editions.

The mental illness model has been stretched in many directions, including the diagnosis of what we see as criminal behaviour. This use has a robust history reaching back in time well before the first *DSM* appeared in 1952. People who have done criminal or evil things are often described as sick or ill. When the morality of a person's actions is questioned, they may be described as crazy or insane. However, emotional distress and evil are entirely different things. They may overlap at times in the same person, of course. But it says something about the 'crazy' label that it takes on so many meanings; it has become a catch-all to push aside things we may struggle to face in ourselves.

Evil is one of many things that may be hard for us to look at without averting our eyes. When we recoil over the evil that we can do, it does seem that it must be craziness. Questioning our own discomfort, questioning what may be a reflection of something ugly within us, is a challenge that is more easily ignored by putting it in a box. Put it over there. That is not me. That is an illness that should be treated, medicated, perhaps even locked away. It is a convenient misdirection that can keep us feeling safe, clean and good. But you do not have to be mentally 'ill' or 'criminally insane' to do evil things. The diagnostic model of mental illness simply allows us an out. If we see something we don't like or that we think of as bad, it can be categorised as an illness and explained in a safe way. But does a diagnostic listing in the *DSM* make it a real or true thing? Perhaps we would do better to first question ourselves. What would it mean, instead, to confront human distress and evil acts without shoving them into a 'crazy box' that we can separate from ourselves? What would it mean to confront evil without flinching, knowing the potential for it is always within us, perhaps not so far from the surface? What would it mean to look at trauma, pain and loss and accept our own very real vulnerability to the events experienced by people sitting right in front of us, without having to look away?

When I was sitting for the oral examination for registration as a psychologist in Ontario, one of the examiners asked me, 'How does a client-centred therapist come to terms with diagnosis?' I honestly can't remember exactly how I answered, although I do remember being relieved by the question. It is a thoughtful, relevant and interesting question, and one that has remained with me all these years. If I reflect on it now, I would say, to begin with, that I have an uneasy relationship with diagnosis as it is used in psychology and psychiatry. The uneasiness comes from the tension I feel in recognising that diagnosis can be both helpful and harmful in powerful ways. Living with and coming to understand this tension has been an ongoing part of my professional development. I was 'raised' as client-centred over many years, so diagnosis simply wasn't part of my upbringing. We spent our time trying to understand people directly and as free of theory as possible, staying focused on what they were expressing or needing in the moment, what they were describing about their unique experiences. I have also worked in other settings where diagnosis was assumed to be part of the natural course of things, integral to what psychologists do when we work with people. I hold these contradictory influences in me.

Some people do all they can to run from diagnosis. Others seek out a diagnosis and receive it with relief; having a label for their distress gives them a sense that they are not alone, that someone understands them. In many insurance, healthcare and educational systems, a diagnosis may unlock much-needed benefits, treatments and supports. A diagnosis also objectifies the person being diagnosed and can create a barrier to seeing the other person more fully as an individual whose suffering is unique to them. I am reminded of William Osler, the Canadian physician considered by many to be the father of modern medicine. Osler insisted that, in order to learn medicine, students had to actually meet and talk with the people they saw as patients. Yes, that was once a radical idea. He is credited with saying, 'The good physician treats the disease; the great physician treats the patient who has the disease.' Osler perfectly expressed one of the essential problems of diagnosis – that we can fall readily into seeing and treating diagnoses and not people, effectively objectifying and alienating the people we work with, making them into 'others' and dehumanising them. We can too easily make people into problems. It is against this complex backdrop that I diagnose.

Diagnosis is part of my daily work, and it still sits uneasily with me. In Ontario, where I practise, the power to diagnose is restricted by law to a few regulated health professions, and psychology is among them. This restriction implies a recognition of the potential to harm other people by diagnosing them incorrectly. It also implies that such a potentially harmful act requires great caution and the acquisition of specialised knowledge, training and experience. Under the law in Ontario, it is referred to as a 'controlled act'. However, its potential for becoming an *act of control* is rarely examined. I rarely hear colleagues enter into discussion about this, expressing concern over how they may be dehumanising other people while trying to help them.

Over the years, I have seen diagnosis misused countless times as the rationale for ordering a chemical straitjacket. Psychiatrists medicated people deemed by facility staff to be disruptive in some way, usually because they were loud, unco-operative or frightening to someone. I met a great many people who carried diagnoses of schizophrenia or schizo-affective disorder who were more probably suffering the effects of a stroke or dementia and had been locked away in a chronic-care facility. Even more frequently, I worked with people given these diagnostic labels whose functional and intelligence levels would be consistent with our current conceptualisation of developmental disabilities. Their ability to express distress was very basic: they would tantrum and then they would be sent to the psychiatrist to have their medication changed. When I chatted with them, it was not unusual for them to describe their thoughts, including their upsetting thoughts, as voices. This is also what others taught them – that their thoughts were voices, that they were psychotic and that they needed medication to stop these voices. They readily believed that they were hallucinating, that they were crazy, because they heard voices. I still wonder about the impact of their diagnoses and subsequent years of medication – did this create actual disorder beyond their emotional distress and inability to express it beyond the level of a tantrum?

Having spent a lot of time with people in a number of chronic care facilities, I also observed that some doctors have a tendency to gravitate towards favourite diagnoses. One psychiatrist almost always diagnosed people with schizo-affective disorder; another almost always diagnosed people with paranoid schizophrenia. I once worked on a ward in which almost all of the women were diagnosed with borderline personality disorder – histrionic personality disorder was apparently going out of style, although I did see this diagnosis on charts from time to time. Almost all of the men in this same facility were diagnosed with narcissistic personality disorder or anti-social personality disorder. In all of these places, the staff came to see the people they were working with as defined by their diagnostic labels, and this seemed to guide their interactions. Treatment was largely reduced to medications that ensured good behaviour and a quiet unit.

Unfortunately, health professionals are not the only ones who fall prey to this kind of thinking. People experiencing chronic pain often tell me that their family members diagnose them. One woman suffering with chronic pain described her irritability and tendency to get angry quickly with others when her pain was worse. She told me that her family would respond to her outbursts by calling her 'bipolar'. She became worried that they might be right. Their relationships became increasingly defined by this diagnostic frame that her family imposed on her. It became a real barrier to their ability to see her suffering more fully and accurately, and it alienated her, even in her own home. She simply had become 'crazy', allowing everyone to move on and not really listen to her; to not really accept her experience of suffering with chronic pain.

I also once worked on a locked unit in which there was an 'outbreak' of multiple personality disorder. The diagnosis came from the people who were there for treatment. They approached staff with news of their multiple personalities and what they were saying, doing or planning. They seemed to be alienated, isolated and needing some kind of human connection and attention that they were not getting from staff, even if it came in the form of inevitable changes in their medication or treatment plans or in the form of a reaction, a response from another human being that acknowledged they were there.

Diagnosis carries the power of authority, an institutional backing, which can also reinforce bigotry at an individual level. This may be seen in diagnoses that are used to control women, such as borderline and histrionic personality disorder. Histrionic personality disorder, of course, has its etymological roots in the notion that a woman could be in distress, driven mad perhaps, because of a wandering uterus. Seriously, I could not make this stuff up if I tried. It is an absurd but true origin story that helps to explain why it is so rare to see a man carry this diagnosis that was most certainly defined by men. Matthew B Ryan, a client-centred colleague of mine, has pointed out:

An important thing to keep in mind about 'hysteria' is that, while the clinical sense of the word has commonly been used to diminish and negate women's lived experiences, the popular sense of the word has commonly been used to diminish and negate women's lived experiences. (Personal communication)

I have seen histrionic personality disorder diagnosed with decreasing frequency over the years, but even a cursory examination reveals the discomfort it expresses with women's power, sexuality and experience, and in particular a discomfort with women who are comfortable with expressing any of these.

Currently the diagnosis I see increasingly used to control women and invalidate their experiences of trauma and shut them up is borderline personality disorder. I find it remarkable how many women who have suffered severe traumas are diagnosed as borderline, when what clinicians should be addressing is the trauma they have experienced and how they live with the impact of it in a society that prefers not to believe them, that would rather they were silenced, and prefers to blame them for the harms inflicted on them. I have frequently encountered women diagnosed as borderline who have experienced traumas that were prolonged and horrific. Just as in Freud's day, we still really don't talk much about this in polite society. The decision to diagnose a woman as borderline, to say she has a characterological problem rather than recognise her trauma, and our societal failure to offer support for her emotional distress, are deeply disturbing. The diagnosis of borderline personality disorder carries deep meaning and has a real impact on how we interact with people who have been given it as a defining label.

In the first *DSM*, homosexuality found its way into the diagnosis of sexual deviation as a pathologic behaviour. It may be worth considering the entire diagnostic description:

> This diagnosis is reserved for deviant sexuality which is not symptomatic of more extensive syndromes, such as schizophrenic and obsessional reactions. The term includes most of the cases formerly classified as 'psychopathic personality and pathologic sexuality'. The diagnosis will specify the type of the pathologic behavior, such as homosexuality, transvestitism, pedophilia, fetishism and sexual sadism (including rape, sexual assault, mutilation). (American Psychiatric Association, 1952: 38–39)

Let that sink in for a moment. 'Homosexuals' were diagnosed as 'deviants', seen in the same way as those who committed horrible and dehumanising criminal acts, 'including rape, sexual assault, mutilation'. Homosexuality was given an upgrade in the form of its own diagnostic category in *DSM-II* (American Psychiatric Association, 1968). It was then replaced with the diagnosis of 'sexual orientation disturbance' in *DSM-III* (American Psychiatric Association, 1980), and classified as ego-dystonic homosexuality. This change moved the diagnosis in the direction of defining homosexuality as a disorder only if a person was unhappy being 'homosexual'. For anyone who understands homophobia and internalised homophobia, this is not much of an improvement. In fact, it is in a subtle but different way just as damaging. It conveys the idea that, in a homophobic society, it is the 'homosexual' person who is in need of treatment, rather than society that needs to change. *DSM-III-R* (American Psychiatric Association, 1987) buried the diagnosis a bit further, but it could still be found under 'sexuality disorder not otherwise specified', along with the words 'persistent and marked distress about one's sexual orientation'. In the late 1980s, when I was struggling with coming out and during the brief turmoil shortly after I came out, I would have carried this diagnostic label. I am 'homosexual', a diagnosable disorder grouped with violent criminality in *DSM-I* parlance, but it seems that the *DSM* gave me a miracle cure in 1994, when *DSM-IV* (American Psychiatric Association) removed references to homosexuality as a disorder altogether.

While this diagnosis no longer exists, the equally disturbing transphobic diagnosis of gender identity disorder, which first appeared in *DSM-III*, continues to find life as gender dysphoria disorder in *DSM-5* (American Psychiatric Association, 2013). What makes a trans identity a disorder, according to *DSM-5*, is strikingly familiar if we care enough to pay attention to the history of diagnostic categories: 'The condition is associated with clinically significant distress or impairment in social, occupational, or other important areas of functioning' (p453). Not only is being trans seen as a 'condition', but it is distress about being trans that marks it as a disorder. Apparently being transphobic is not a condition. For that matter, not being trans is also apparently not a condition. Again, we are faced with a diagnostic category that places the focus on distress experienced by the individual experiencing harm in our society, rather than turning our lens towards a transphobic society that an individual is living within and dealing with every day. The focus is turned away from a society still very much in need of growth and change.

The existence of such a diagnosis reflects an institutionally sanctioned transphobia. The further danger is that the views of a transphobic clinician are thus reinforced by their profession; they have a rationale to 'treat' or 'cure' trans people, while those in society who are not trans are let off the hook for their part in reinforcing the transphobic conditions that cause a healthy individual to suffer. It says a great deal about our diagnostic framework of mental illnesses that there is no diagnosis for racism, sexism, homophobia, transphobia, anti-semitism, ageism, ableism or a more global bigoted personality disorder, with sub-classifications and the flexibility to diagnose its traits. Instead, it is the people who are most directly harmed by these societal problems who carry diagnostic labels and on whom treatment efforts and attempts to control are focused. The real disorders in society go unseen and undiagnosed. The perspective of time allows us to have more courage to be curious about and question the diagnostic categories in the current *DSM*. Indeed, after taking a historical tour of the *DSM* formulations regarding sexual identity back to 1952, it is hard not to say, 'Wow, what a load of crap.'

As we reflect on the way diagnosis dehumanises, we may wonder if there is any way out, aside from moving beyond the act of diagnosing. It seems unlikely that we will any time soon find ourselves in a world that no longer assumes a need for diagnosis, at least with respect to the experience of distress. So, in the meantime, is there a way to live with the diagnostic system and not dehumanise others, while advocating for change? I am a cautious optimist, and I like to think the answer is a somewhat attenuated yes. It is an immense task and it begins, but does not end, with each of us. I believe it is incumbent on each of us to look at the act of diagnosis squarely, including our relationship to it, what it does to other people and what it does to us. How do we misuse diagnosis? How do our personal discomforts get in the way of recognising our misuse of these labels, which has so much potential to harm others?

The question I was once asked during my orals, 'How does a client-centred therapist come to terms with diagnosis?' is a question that is relevant to all clinicians. What is our understanding of the diagnostic process and the diagnostic labels we use? What is the history of those labels and do we find ourselves able to recognise that our current usage will some day be part of an outdated understanding that will make future clinicians uncomfortable, just as many constructs in *DSM-I* seem so implausible or ludicrous today? Our modern and seemingly enlightened present can easily become a future clinician's historical curiosity, a past riddled with dehumanising concepts that are seen more clearly for what they are. Studying history is indeed humbling when applied to the present, to our still limited knowledge in the fields of psychology and psychiatry, and to ourselves.

We have had four *DSM*s since the 1952 edition, along with a revision (*DSM-III-R*) and a text revision (*DSM-IV-TR*). *DSM-5*, published in 2013, now uses Arabic numerals instead of Roman, so that the publishers can produce updated versions similar to Microsoft updates: *DSM-5.1*, *DSM-5.2* etc. This suggests that the new frame of *DSM-5* may be with us for a while, but changes may occur to the diagnostic categories. Some diagnoses have been added and others removed. Some disorders have been gradually transformed. The diagnostic criteria for post-traumatic stress disorder, for example, have changed in the move from *DSM-IV-TR* to *DSM-5*. Technically, this means that someone who carried this diagnosis pre-2013 might not carry it according to *DSM-5*. It would seem obvious, on casual reflection, that the nature of human distress is relatively constant, despite the many changes in *DSM* that attempt to describe or categorise it.

When we look closer and reflect on the realities people share with us on an ongoing basis, diagnoses of emotional distress all appear to be variations of an 'adjustment disorder' – a difficulty adapting in the face of a stressor, challenge or loss. Diagnostic categories have been developed in part to aid research into the effectiveness of treatment or prevention efforts. The criteria must allow for clear differentiation of types of distress, typically grouping symptoms that appear to occur together. However, these criterion sets that are used to describe a syndrome may not reflect the messier realities of individual experiences and expressions of distress when we encounter people in our work. Research is also conducted by excluding people who do not neatly fit into the *DSM* diagnostic box that is being examined. This is often a very real limitation of the body of research in our field that may go ignored. Most people who sit with me in my office present with a complex tapestry of distressing thoughts and feelings that are in flux and may meet criteria for multiple diagnoses. They typically do not fit neatly in one diagnostic box, and the distress does not sit cleanly in distinct places in their brains, as if they were separate chapters of the *DSM*. It is worth regularly considering and reminding ourselves what diagnoses are. Diagnoses can point to something real beyond them and may or may not be useful guiding stories, but they are not real in and of themselves. Diagnoses are theoretical; distress and impairment are not.

Despite the benefits of diagnosis, and to borrow the medical model many of us seem so comfortable with, we face a very real pandemic in the healthcare professions in relation to working with people in distress. I would even say that our field suffers from a diagnosis disorder – or, more accurately, I think most clinicians suffer from this disorder. When we come to question this in ourselves, our answers, responses, actions or lack thereof, will determine whether humanisation is possible. With this in mind, I close this chapter with my proposal for a new diagnostic category to be considered in the next iteration of the *DSM*. It is likely to be met with something less than approval, which perhaps is diagnostic. I offer the following for your consideration and reflection.

Diagnosis Disorder

Diagnostic Criteria:

    A. One or both of the following:

        1. The clinician diagnoses distress experienced by other people as a mental disorder.

2. The clinician sees diagnostic labels of distress as real or true things, in and of themselves.

B. These symptoms are clinically significant, as evidenced by any of the following, based on observation or subjective report:

1. The clinician treats the diagnosis and not the individual (evidence for this may be seen in treatment plans developed entirely on the basis of a diagnosis with no consideration of individual contextual factors. Evidence may also be seen in the rejection of treatment for individuals not meeting full diagnostic criteria for a disorder).

2. The clinician is unable to see alternatives to diagnostic labels as ways of describing distress (such as the narrative of the individual experiencing the distress).

3. The clinician is unable to recognise the source or cause of distress experienced by the patient as being reinforced by societal forms of oppression.

4. The clinician applies a diagnosis without considering all available sources of information, including a full encounter with the individual in distress.

5. The clinician feels discomfort engaging in treatment without a diagnostic label. In some instances, the clinician may feel entirely unable to do so.

6. The clinician does not recognise the limits of diagnosis.

7. Being questioned about the act of diagnosis or about the reality of diagnostic categories causes distress for the clinician. (This may be seen in defensiveness, especially towards the person offering this diagnosis. The clinician may take offence at being diagnosed with this disorder. Related to this is the tendency to see any theoretical concepts as truth.)

Specifiers:

Specify if:

Ego-syntonic: the clinician making diagnoses has no discomfort when doing so (this typically is a worse prognostic indicator).

Ego-dystonic: the clinician making diagnoses is conflicted when doing so.

Specify current severity:

Mild: the clinician recognises the harm that can be done by diagnosing and is able to recognise the patient's distress from the patient's perspective, but still diagnoses and/or believes that diagnostic labels are real things.

Moderate: the number and intensity of symptoms is between mild and severe.

Severe: a pervasive pattern of symptoms is present that interferes significantly with the clinician's ability to recognise the distress the patient experiences from the patient's perspective.

Diagnostic Features: the essential features of a diagnosis disorder are the inability to see the emotional distress experienced by other people from their own lived perspective and a belief that diagnostic labels are necessary and adequately explain the distress experienced by others.

Associated Features Supporting Diagnosis: diagnosis disorder is associated with concrete thinking and difficulty thinking outside of the box. An inability to accept contrary viewpoints may be present. In severe cases, it is difficult to separate this disorder from a narcissistic personality.

Prevalence: while epidemiological studies have not yet been undertaken, the number of those who diagnose and who carry this diagnosis is thought to be of pandemic proportions.

Development and Course: an inability to question oneself and broader belief systems, as well as a tendency to take oneself too seriously, are often seen as precursors. While the seeds of this disorder are thought to be present more generally in society, this disorder is commonly reinforced through graduate training across healthcare professions. Its typical progress can be charted in relation to years of experience in the field and practice in carrying out diagnosis.

Risk and Prognostic Factors: the risk for this disorder increases with the number of degrees earned in post-secondary education.

The prognosis worsens as the number of symptoms increases. The number of years carrying out diagnosis correlates positively with an increasingly worse prognosis. When this disorder is ego-syntonic, the prognosis is particularly grim.

Culture-Related Diagnostic Issues: once a clinician is diagnosed with this disorder, there appear to be no cultural differences in its expression.

Gender-Related Diagnostic Issues: although there is no actual research to date, it is thought that there is little difference in the nature of this disorder when broken down by gender.

Differential Diagnosis: there is significant overlap with the diagnostic criteria of a number of disorders listed in *DSM* that may also be co-morbid with diagnosis disorder. Recognising the occurrence of the act of diagnosing and the belief in diagnostic categories as real things is important. The following are some of the most common differential diagnoses to consider: delusional disorder, narcissistic personality disorder, anti-social personality disorder; other specified mental disorder; unspecified mental disorder.

References

American Psychiatric Association (2013). *Diagnostic and Statistical Manual of Mental Disorders* (5th ed). Washington, DC: American Psychiatric Publishing.

American Psychiatric Association (1994). *Diagnostic and Statistical Manual of Mental Disorders* (4th ed). Washington, DC: American Psychiatric Publishing.

American Psychiatric Association (1987). *Diagnostic and Statistical Manual of Mental Disorders* (3rd ed, revised). Washington, DC: American Psychiatric Publishing.

American Psychiatric Association (1980). *Diagnostic and Statistical Manual of Mental Disorders* (3rd ed). Washington, DC: American Psychiatric Publishing.

American Psychiatric Association (1968). *Diagnostic and Statistical Manual of Mental Disorders* (2nd ed). Washington, DC: American Psychiatric Publishing.

American Psychiatric Association (1952). *Diagnostic and Statistical Manual of Mental Disorders*. Washington, DC: American Psychiatric Association.

Freire P (1994). *Pedagogy of the Oppressed* (20th anniversary ed.) New York, NY: Continuum.

Osler W (undated). *Osler's Aphorisms*. [Online.] The Osler Club of London. www.osler.org.uk/osleriana-2/oslers-aphorisms/ (accessed 17 November 2018).

Szasz TS (2010). *The Myth of Mental Illness: foundations of a theory of personal conduct*. New York, NY: HarperCollins.

6

Personality-by-numbers

Understanding is but the sum of our misunderstandings.
Sumire (Murakami, 2001: 134)

I had a paint-by-numbers kit when I was a child – a white canvas board with a patchwork of odd shapes thinly outlined in a dull grey-blue. Dull grey-blue numbers sat roughly in the middle of each outlined shape, each number corresponding to a paint colour. I carefully and dutifully filled in the shapes with the correct paint colour according to its number. When I was finished, I had a painting that reasonably resembled a basset hound. But something was missing, something beyond the numbers.

Today, as a registered psychologist, I have a large collection of testing kits, each with a test that has its own way of leading to a set of numbers and a manual that tells me what the numbers are supposed to mean. It's all in the numbers: intelligence quotients, raw scores, standard scores, t-scores, z-scores, means, standard deviations, scale scores, subscale scores, cut scores, validity index scores, supplemental validity index scores, clinical scale scores and profile configurations. The numbers indicate how intelligent someone is. The numbers tell us if someone is depressed, and how depressed they are. The numbers tell us if someone is anxious and how anxious they are. The numbers tell us about a person's personality, how 'resistant' they may be to treatment, and even whether they might be a good police officer. The numbers also tell us if a person is exaggerating their distress or their problems with thinking, concentration and memory.

At least that is the theory, and the test manuals tell us so. Test publishers imply that the numbers will give us truth. It is a pretty song, and many of us sing along while ignoring other melodies, including caveats that are noted clearly in the manuals. It would be nice if it really were so simple, if all we have to do is give a person some tests and we can then rely on the numbers alone to give us all the answers we need. Unfortunately, the numbers may not always be telling us what we think they are telling us.

At the turn of the last century, in France, a man named Alfred Binet developed what would become the model, in many ways, for the development of tests of cognitive functioning – a battery of tests that quantified various brain functions and allowed for comparison of the results with samples of people from the general population. Binet's test battery is an important milestone in the history of test construction and statistical analysis applied to people in an effort to use science to understand them. An updated version of his test is still in use and I was trained in its use during my first practical training in diagnostic assessment as a doctoral student. Binet's test also established the practice of standardising procedures in order to enhance the reliability of the results. It has since been overshadowed by the Wechsler Scales, a battery of aptitude tests that were first developed during World War Two, again using a standardised approach and allowing for comparison of the results with large groups of people. Today aptitude tests are used for many purposes – as part of a larger battery of tests for assessing brain injury and disease, as a tool to aid in placement decisions for special education programmes, as a source of information about potential learning disabilities, in vocational assessments to determine aptitudes relevant to occupational tasks, and as a basic measure of behaviour under controlled conditions.

Aptitude tests are, of course, not without controversy. We are increasingly aware of the limits of interpretation when using tests of cognitive functioning, particularly as we are also becoming increasingly aware of the inescapable impact of culture and language and how poorly these may be accounted for in the numbers we end up with after administering our tests. To complicate matters, it does not take a great deal of intelligence to determine the wrong answers and score poorly on a test on purpose. It also doesn't take much imagination to recognise that someone could attempt to score poorly on a test in order to gain some sort of benefit. To my knowledge, no one documented the first time this subterfuge was recognised but it's likely that this anonymous event occurred quite early in the history of psychological testing. It likely has occurred quite often since then. Over time, psychologists have gone about developing tests to detect this possibility of deceit. These tests have undergone refinements over the years and we find ourselves currently with an abundance of such measures, which we now call performance validity tests, or effort tests. Unfortunately, the way the results are interpreted is not always logical, although we dutifully follow what the test manuals and research literature tell us about how to interpret the scores to detect people who are faking. Essentially, we use deception in an effort to detect deception. But in the end, we are often really only measuring the adequacy of someone's effort, not deceit.

The most common format for these tests to detect deception is described as forced choice. Test items require a choice of A or B, with items that are generally easy and should yield a very high number of correct responses. In this regard, I can clearly recall a woman I once assessed who had a mild developmental disability, yet she achieved a perfect score on every trial of a performance validity test. Research studies are conducted to set a reasonable level, called a cut score, below which it is thought that the person taking the test is not giving adequate effort. What this means is that we cannot reliably interpret the rest of our tests of cognitive functioning if a performance measure indicates inadequate effort. The cut score is above the range of scores that can occur due to statistical chance. When someone is simply guessing and not really engaging in the task, they are likely to produce scores in the chance range. When someone scores in the chance range, we cannot say they were doing so deliberately in an effort to look impaired. However, if a person scores below statistical chance on a forced choice test, they are very likely to be trying to choose the wrong answers. But there may be many reasons for this.

Test manuals tell us that when a score is below the cut-off, we cannot interpret the rest of our test data in a meaningful way. This is very reasonable. However, it is commonly stated that a score below the cut-off indicates feigning, or malingering. In other words, the person taking the test is being deceptive. And this is where I have some disagreement. A score in the grey area between the cut score and the low end of a reasonable chance range only indicates, at best, that a person's effort was inadequate. This could be for many reasons, including random guessing or engaging well enough to get the right answer some of the time while disengaging and simply guessing at other times. Such behaviour can hardly be described across the board as an attempt at faking impairment. Put another way, a score that is consistent with random guessing is far from conclusive evidence of an effort to look impaired.

A test manual may instruct us, when someone scores below a cut score, to note in our reports that this score is even lower than scores typically achieved, for example, by people with dementia or those with developmental disabilities. The unsupported implication carried by this sort of statement is obvious: the person scoring this low must be faking their impairment. Some test manuals state that we should see this as evidence of malingering. But painting with a broad brushstroke based on a number and using a colour chosen by the test developer ignores the multitude of meanings that may be present in a number that lies in the grey area below the cut score but still within a reasonable range of chance. As I have explained, a person who is distracted, disinterested or just wants to finish as quickly as possible may guess, sometimes frequently, resulting in a score below the cut-off. With this awareness, comparing this person by score to a person with dementia or a developmental disability who engaged adequately is disingenuous and manipulative. At best the comparison is ill-conceived.

Even when someone scores below random chance, suggesting they attempted to look impaired, things may not be as simple as they appear. It is only reasonable to assume scores below random chance are achieved purposely. However, it is an error to equate intentionally poor performance on a forced choice test with lack of impairment. Someone may be attempting to score poorly out of anger, for example, or because of poor judgement. I worked with a person who dropped out of school early because of a learning disability. School made him feel judged as stupid by others. He set out on his own path outside of the school system and became a very successful businessman. Unfortunately, he sustained a brain injury and came to our clinic for an assessment to determine his impairments. Part of this assessment was a standard day of neuropsychological testing, including effort tests.

He participated in the day of testing, and his scores on the effort tests were well below the low end of a reasonable chance range. In other words, it was clear that he deliberately failed the tests. When I spoke with him afterwards, he acknowledged this. He explained that he was angry with the examiner because it felt like he was in school again and being told he was stupid. So, he decided to teach the examiner a lesson and do as poorly as possible and respond with ridiculous answers. I had to spend time talking with him to get this very important and honest story that placed the numbers in a meaningful context.

Someone may also be attempting to score poorly because they don't trust us to do an adequate job of recognising their impairments. Simply asking the people we work with to trust us to get it right is not likely to be a sound strategy to get past what may be significant and often understandable trust issues. Some communities have been on the receiving end of atrocities committed by health professionals they were supposed to trust. Here I offer a few words: the Tuskegee Syphilis Study. Chances are, unless you are African American, you don't know why these words are meaningful, especially in the context of this chapter. I am referring to the infamous study that was carried out by the United States Public Health Service on African American men over a period of 40 years (Centers for Disease Control and Prevention, 2015). In this study, the men were told they would receive, among other things, free healthcare from the government for participating. Disturbingly, the real purpose of the study was to observe the natural course of untreated syphilis, not to treat it. None of the men in this study were told they had syphilis, and while treatment with penicillin was known to be effective and was readily available, none was given.

In the face of such real and horrible events as the Tuskegee Syphilis Study, even if you believe yourself to be trustworthy, it is naïve to believe all of the people you work with will accept that you are trustworthy just because you tell them so. Despite what the test manuals tell us, the numbers cannot tell us what a person's motives were for how they engaged in testing. Even if the numbers are below chance levels, we don't know why a person was motivated to answer questions incorrectly. Deceit? Anger? Poor judgement? Confusion? Lack of trust? The only reasonable and honest conclusion we can draw is whether enough effort was made to allow us to interpret the rest of our test data in a meaningful way.

Another interesting hypothesis is that a failed performance validity test may be a statistical aberration, an anomaly. In other words, the person taking the test was just unusually unlucky with their guesses. To address this possibility, some psychologists have proposed using two or three different performance validity measures. If someone then fails all of these measures, the thinking goes, it can be assumed they were feigning their cognitive impairment. However, if someone simply does not engage well during testing, there is no reason why more performance validity measures would necessarily result in a different outcome. In fact, we may be sampling the same disengaged behaviours over and over again.

Erin Bigler (2015) has suggested that scores below the cut off but not below the range of random chance may be the product of symptoms associated with various disorders. As long as scores are still statistically within the range of random chance, it cannot be asserted that someone intended to do poorly. This is where critical thinking is critical. Applying research findings and test manual instructions without critical thinking is potentially misleading and dangerous. By applying the numbers concretely, without considering a broader context, we may be stating a truth that tells a lie. The numbers are always part of a broader story that we can only begin to know by going down other paths, such as actually talking to people themselves to help us place the numbers in context. After all of the tests have been scored, I have made it my routine practice to explore in an open-ended fashion what people experienced during testing, in order to learn more about what the numbers might mean.

So far, I have only addressed the numbers we get from tests of cognitive functioning. But our psychological paint-by-numbers kits are vast. We also have tests that help us consider personality factors and symptoms of emotional distress and their severity. Freud used dream interpretation as a means to unlock the secrets of the mind in an effort to make unconscious conflicts conscious and to bring about change. This individualised approach is time-consuming compared with today's psychological tests that can be administered rapidly and en masse. However, it has the advantage of being highly personal and conforming to a more intimate knowledge of the individual person's context as it unfolds in psychoanalysis. Jung's word-association test served a similar purpose, asking people to say the first word that comes to mind in response to words offered by the psychoanalyst.

During World War Two, Stark Hathaway and JC McKinley did for personality testing what Binet did for tests of cognitive functioning. Their work was carried out at the University of Minnesota, the same university that was home to Paul Meehl, ground zero for the explosion and widespread Newtonian fallout that continues to influence the field. In 1943, Hathaway and McKinley published the Minnesota Multiphasic Personality Inventory, or MMPI for short – the most researched and widely used psychological test of symptom presentation and personality features, if we include all of its incarnations. The test carries the perfect brand name coming out of the massive military industrial complex of the World War Two-era United States. It allows an efficient, mass-production approach to personality assessment based on research that correlates various symptoms and personality traits with answers to true/false test items, which often appear on the surface to have no relevance to what is being measured. This inventory of symptoms and personality features is a ship's manifest, and it is a behemoth of a ship. It houses an impossibly large cargo of human personalities reduced to numbers and combinations of numbers. It is the quintessential test that captured the Newtonian imaginations and aspirations of our field; it sets out to diagnose a person, explain them, and describe their personality, with numbers generated by responses to hundreds of true/false items and the application of statistics.

The creation of the MMPI is a watershed event in the field of psychology. It has inspired the creation of countless tests. Our alphabet soup of personality and symptom severity tests is indeed mind-boggling: BAI, BDI-II, BHI-2, BHS, CORE-OM, CORE-10, GAD-7, MMPI, MMPI-2, MMPI-2A, MMPI-2RF, PAI, PHQ-9, MCMI-IV, MBTI, SCII, 16PF, and so on. You would be hard-pressed to find a reasonably conducted assessment for legal purposes that does not include some of the more robust measures available to us and that does not consider the numbers they generate. Just as with cognitive tests, these tests are vulnerable to deception on the part of the person taking them. The more complex tests have built-in measures to assess a person's response style. For all sorts of reasons, subtle and obvious, people may try either to minimise or hide their distress or exaggerate or over-report it. And, just as we have a multitude of standalone effort tests for use with tests of cognitive functioning, we have a substantial acronymed arsenal of standalone tests designed specifically to assess for exaggeration of emotional distress: MFAST, SIMS, SIRS, and SIRS-

2, just to name some. With all of these, our trusted test manuals tell us how to interpret the numbers to determine if someone is exaggerating, minimising, inconsistent etc.

Many clinicians hold fast to the numbers without considering the context offered by all the other sources of information that may be available. Some will even say they cannot diagnose when test scores are invalid, or they cannot determine how impaired someone is. The numbers have become king, and all of our clinical training and critical thinking is rendered, somehow, irrelevant in the face of numbers. If a number on a test suggests that a person is exaggerating or faking, other, often compelling sources of information are ignored. However, as with effort tests, there is a story beyond the numbers. Context is everything.

Two of the most widely accepted and respected psychological tests in forensic (legal) contexts are the MMPI-2RF and the PAI. With respect to the MMPI-2RF, one of the test developers, Yossef Ben-Porath (2012), frequently states that the validity scores should be interpreted in the context of 'extra-test data', such as a detailed medical and psychological history. In other words, the test score on its own is insufficient to draw a conclusion, as a number of interpretations are possible and consistent with these scores. Leslie Morey, the developer of the PAI, similarly asserts:

> Diagnostic and screening decisions should never be based exclusively on the results of the PAI. Such decisions necessarily require multiple sources of information, which may include, but are not limited to, (a) case histories and other historical data; (b) the results of mental status exams and clinical interview; and (c) the results of projective, neuropsychological, intelligence, cognitive ability, and other self-report measures. (2007: 7)

Despite such clear statements about the importance of not relying solely on test scores, it remains commonplace, whether in assessment or treatment work. Tests are frequently seen as time-savers, a quick way to get some answers. Computer programmes can even offer rather elaborate narratives about who the test-taker is, giving the impression of a thoughtful interpretation of the data when psychologists quote them in their work. However, these interpretations cannot be relied upon without question, and must be considered within the context of all of our other sources of information. It simply is not good practice for clinicians to rely solely on computer-generated interpretations that are based on numbers. While we end up with something that reasonably resembles a person, something is missing. Something beyond the numbers.

Whether the tests are standalone or integrated into a larger test, the purpose of symptom validity testing is to determine someone's response style: are they being straightforward, exaggerating, responding inappropriately, or holding back? These determinations are made through a statistical analysis of the person's responses in comparison with the responses of patient and non-patient ('normative') groups analysed in numerous research studies. When we make statements about someone's test scores, we are comparing them with samples of other people who essentially define what is normal with respect to what is being measured. Interpretation of the scale scores that we look at to determine someone's response style are based on these normative groups, so when we are interpreting them, we are assuming the person taking the test is like these groups. Unfortunately, that is often not the case. We make interpretations as if the normative sample is always representative of test-takers who come to see us, despite a potential lack of fit. What if a person is not normal in the sense of not sharing enough in common with the normative samples? There are many ways that people may not fit the normative landscape of a test. I often find that the following merit investigation and consideration: language, culture, and a potentially idiosyncratic way of reading the items.

Some test manuals encourage further analysis of answers when the validity scales indicate inconsistent responding. Inconsistent responding refers to people responding differently to items with similar meanings, which means we can't rely on the scores to mean anything. When inconsistent responding is flagged, there are a number of possible reasons, and that is why follow-up is such an obvious and important recommendation. A person could be confused, have reading comprehension issues, or have difficulty concentrating over the time it takes to complete the entire test. The reasons are often as individual as the people taking these tests, and follow-up yields meaningful context beyond the numbers. What one person told me reflected their occasionally random and disengaged responding: 'There were so many [questions] and some were difficult.

I didn't really think on all of them, I just wanted to mark something down.' Another person had difficulty with vocabulary and reading comprehension and became angry while completing one of the tests of symptom severity. I asked her later about her experience and how she understood the questions, and she said: 'I was going to throw the questions out the window. I don't understand them, they're stupid questions. I'm not saying I'm a dumb-ass, but people my age know this word and I don't. Why don't I know this word? It really upsets you. It just upsets you.' Interestingly, inconsistency can cut both ways when it comes to reading comprehension. Here is what another person told me about her experience of test items, which are supposed to be written at the reading level of a 10-year-old: 'They don't make these tests with intelligent people in mind. There were a lot of questions asked twice but asked just ever so differently. So, because they were asked differently, I had a different response. And maybe after answering 20 questions and thinking harder about it, then OK, maybe this instead of that when I'm asked again. And then it's too tiring to go back and change the other answers.'

Some tests of symptom severity and personality functioning also include a scale based on items that are infrequently endorsed, and some tests manuals suggest that we also explore these infrequent responses to learn what they may indicate. Typically, these items are rather ridiculous or bizarre, and when someone endorses them it raises the possibility of carelessness, random responding or reading difficulties. Someone with a naïve understanding of psychopathology may also be trying to 'fake crazy'. Again, without further exploration, I am left only with a number, an incomplete truth at best. During a routine follow-up after his testing was scored, I asked a man I was working with: 'You answered true on this item: "I eat rocks for dinner." What did you mean by that?' He responded: 'Huh? Of course, I don't eat rocks. I'd be dead. I must not have been paying attention.'

Some tests also generate what are known as critical items, and test manuals often suggest that we may want to explore further the answers to these. They ask about issues such as suicidality and alcohol misuse, and also indicate potential faking. Going over their answers with people after the tests are scored is a useful practice. It encourages us further to understand that there is always a context for the numbers yielded by our tests. Sometimes that context is entirely ordinary – the person may be simply distracted and not paying attention, and reviewing these items with them reveals this to us. When I asked a man about affirming an item about being watched by aliens, he responded, 'I don't know, maybe I was just in a rush. I'm not being watched by aliens, I'm not going crazy.' Sometimes an item captures something unique about the person responding to it. In response to an item about not seeing colours, one man told me simply, 'I'm colour blind.'

Sometimes responses to these items tell us something about reading comprehension skills, English language skills or simply a different way of understanding the test items. I have encountered people in a highly vulnerable state who have read their personal distress into items that are about something else entirely. When they explain their answers, it is clear that they are not exaggerating or attempting to look 'crazy.' Rather, they are responding to something that was triggered internally and not to the question or item on the test. In these situations, this pattern of responding appears to be pervasive, and it takes time to recognise what happened when the person took the test. Unfortunately, if we were simply to go by the scale scores of all of these people, we would conclude at best that they were exaggerating and at worst that they were faking their distress entirely.

Also, the scales we use to consider validity issues have names, and this adds a layer to our challenge. When we name something, it focuses our thinking, creates a reality and narrows possibilities that perhaps we should be considering. We may mistake a score on a scale for a truth about the person who took the test, simply because of the name of the scale, such as 'fake bad', 'negative impression management' or 'malingering index'. Because manuals tell us the scores on various scales mean something, we may hold to this meaning as the only possible meaning and not consider that another meaning beyond the number or scale name may be closer to truth.

I often encounter context that paints the numbers in an entirely unexpected way. This is why, in addition to asking what items mean to people after I have reviewed the scored results, I usually ask them about their experience with the tests. People who are bi-cultural may be confused as to which cultural perspective to answer from, and this was made clear by an Indian woman I once assessed who speaks 10 languages, including English. She had great difficulty completing the multiple-choice tests of symptom severity, and many critical items were flagged. Others had previously observed that she seemed not to understand basic questions. However, the truth was quite the opposite. This was immediately apparent during interviewing when she was able to respond eloquently to complex questions; clearly, she understood English very well. When I asked her about her experience with the written tests and why others might have concluded that she struggled to answer basic questions, she explained, 'My difficulty with the questions was to understand in what context the questions were asked. Like my hands are warm. Does that mean like strong, like I don't feel weak? So basically, it was trying to compare here what would it mean. But if it were asked back home, this is what I would have answered. But I am not sure what it would be for here. Like, do I like going to dances? And that was completely confusing to me because, back home, I loved dances, like classical dance and dance competitions, and if there is a programme I'd love to watch it. But here it could mean going to a dance at a nightclub with friends, so it was totally confusing. So I leave it, but I say, "yes". But I don't want people to think I'm a nightclub person because that would not fit me, because I have never been to a nightclub.'

Reviewing items in the context of a follow-up interview can be profoundly revealing. A young man who was involved in a traumatic incident came to see me as part of a disability assessment. He endorsed a number of critical items on testing that suggested potential exaggeration or faking of his distress. When I reviewed the results with him, he explained that he saw multiple choice as an offensive way to try to understand his emotional distress, and this influenced his approach to the test items: 'I just fill it out because I feel like I have no choice, but what I want is for someone to sit with me and hear what I'm saying. That's what I want, but no one is really doing that.' In other words, his answers reflected his response to feeling he was being dehumanised and treated like a number; that I was not taking the time to understand him as a human being, person-to-person, in a conversation. He also explained that he attended numerous assessments hoping to receive psychological treatment for his distress and he never felt that he was listened to or understood. He told me: 'I got to the point I don't even want to see no one [for treatment]. They don't hear me, but I gotta hear them. They don't see me, but I gotta see them. They don't come see me, but I gotta see them. They don't know if I ate, if I have money, or even how I got here.' Clearly the true/false or multiple-choice format is restrictive and may be perceived in a number of ways by people completing them, sometimes causing distress and fuelling a sense of mistrust. People who come to us in a state of desperation may be understandably upset or angered by this format.

People may write in the margins of the response sheet, clarifying their choice when faced with the limitations of true/false or multiple-choice options to communicate their experience. They may also write other meaningful comments on these sheets. Further exploration with them tends to be rich, and at the very least a respectful thing to do. Next to an item asking if the reader has thoughts of suicide, one man wrote, 'Fuck you!' Rather than make any assumptions about his comment, I asked him about it. He responded, 'Did I write that? I was probably pissed. In the end it's something that doesn't cross my mind, you know what I mean? It pisses me off to read it over and over again. It hurts my feelings kind of. Like I picture people looking at me, and thinking, "He should kill himself", you know what I mean? Why would you assume something like that when you know what I went through?' His comment in the margin reflected, among other things, resilience in the face of distress and anger that someone might assume he would want to kill himself because of his impairments.

Richard Rogers, often considered the guru of malingering (feigning) research, along with Michael Bagby at the Centres for Addiction and Mental Health in Toronto, developed a structured interview format to explore potential feigning of symptoms. Their test, known as the Structured Interview of Reported Symptoms (SIRS), is designed so that each scale reflects an issue flagged by research as suggestive of feigning. Along with the PAI and MMPI-2/2RF, the SIRS is considered a gold-standard instrument in forensic contexts. Because this is a structured interview format, the clinician must read the items exactly as they appear in the test booklet and score them in a standardised fashion. A determination of whether someone is likely to be responding genuinely or feigning is based on research models, which of course lead to numbers. An obvious downside of a structured interview is that it can be lengthy to administer in addition to our usual interview (about 30 minutes). The developers also recognised that it should be preceded by a long enough interview to allow psychologists to have some context or appreciation for how people communicate with and respond to us.

I like using the SIRS, despite its limitations, as it often helps me to make sense of numbers from other tests that seem strange and difficult to account for. The structured interview format, if used often enough, provides a familiar framework that allows thoughtful clinicians to make observations and recognise meaningful context that may stand out from the responses that we usually encounter. Because of its structured interview format, the test offers an interactional component and a platform for observation. These observations can help highlight such issues as cultural and language factors, as well as confusion, concrete thinking and distractibility, as long as we are listening well. As Yogi Berra is credited with saying, you can observe a lot just by watching. This is a dimension that self-administered written tests do not have and must be made up for by item analysis through follow-up interviewing.

Not long into a SIRS administration, the person I was interviewing told me, 'Sorry, I wasn't concentrating.' Over the course of the interview, she often needed questions repeated. There were also clear language issues. She was sometimes mistaken in her understanding of English vocabulary and would say, 'Oh, is that what it means?' Her concentration diminished and her energy appeared to flag as we continued. She often needed explanations of the meanings of words in order to respond. On another occasion when administering the SIRS, a simple item helped me recognise some of the limits of someone's English language skills and how they might have affected her responses on other questionnaires that usually tap for faking emotional distress. The item was about plants having magical powers and she responded, 'Trees drop leaves in winter. Trees grow leaves in spring. Trees grow fruit. Yes, they are magical.' The way this test is designed, it is also possible to observe patterns of negative thinking, which are common when people are in distress but may result in invalid test scores that suggest exaggeration. If we attend more fully to the people we work with when they respond to our questions during structured interviews such as this, there is much we can learn about why they may be responding in certain ways in this and other contexts. It may be obvious, but I find that it is essential to listen openly and to be curious when we face other people, taking the time to follow up after testing to learn more about the context that numbers are nested within.

Sadly, I am finding that item analysis through follow-up interviewing appears to be a dying art. Perhaps it comes down to a simple fact: painting by numbers is relatively quick and easy, but understanding nuance takes time and effort. Even those of us willing to make the effort may feel we do not have enough time. In the traditional psychological method of assessment, the test data are but one source of information. We also weigh what we learn from interviewing people and people who know them, reviewing file material, and making behavioural observations. While this is a robust approach, it takes time, and it is not always easy making sense of information from different sources that may seem to contradict each other.

Even when clinicians find the time to consider all of these sources of information, they do not often review test data with the people they have seen when trying to make sense of the numbers. This is unfortunate, as there is so much richness in what people are able to tell us about why they responded the way they did. We are able to learn about their attention and concentration, how well or poorly they may be containing their distress, how they experience others and how others see them, and what their experiences have been during treatment and in their efforts to get treatment. We are able to observe their language skills and potential cultural influences. And, if we are called upon to formulate a diagnosis, we are likely to get a fresh and immediate understanding of the nature and severity of someone's distress by what they tell us about their understanding of test items. The Canadian philosopher Marshall McLuhan offered the seemingly simple statement, 'The medium is the message' (1964). When I apply this to our work as psychologists, and in particular to our assessment method, I wonder what our method is saying about what we are actually doing when we elevate psychological test data above all other sources of information available to us. In other words, the method is the message.

The promise of psychological testing, so similar to my childhood paint-by-numbers kit, is a shortcut through complexity. The numbers we consider are based on test theory. The numbers themselves are incomplete facts that go towards informing our evolving theory of another person's experience – a theory based on a theory that is at least as far removed from people's actual lived experiences as personality theory, if not more so. At least with interviewing, an interaction that happens in a live encounter between us and another person, we can check with the other person if it seems they are not understanding our questions or we are not understanding their answers. We can observe when they are responding to something other than the intended meaning behind the questions we are asking and reflect on what might be happening. With test results and no follow-up interviewing, all we have are numbers.

There is very real danger in taking the numbers as reality, when numbers can't tell the truth on their own. Our interpretations, when taken out of context and based only on numbers, are built on a foundation of potential misunderstandings. My experience is that the numbers always sit in a broader context. There is always a story beyond the numbers that isn't just what the manual or computerised programme tells us. Time and again, I find that context is everything. It is too soon for conclusions to be drawn solely from the numbers. I find myself wondering if we have simply become too impatient; are we that much in need of a fast, concrete answer? Are we that uncomfortable with the ambiguity that lies beyond the numbers?

Nuance takes time, and it is important that we are comfortable with taking enough time to see it. It is essential that we find time to seek out sources of information beyond our numbers; take time with the people we see in our work, and value them and their experience. Test results do not give the entire answer, yet they do hold great meaning if we take the time to confront them more fully; if we take the time to go back and re-examine the data with fresh eyes and ask questions. I believe the numbers serve us best when we are curious enough to raise questions about them, explore further, and engage the other person. Questions are the foundation of science and knowledge, not facts, and definitely not incomplete facts that are devoid of context. Ultimately, questioning the numbers, rather than painting by them, may bring us closer to understanding other people and their experiences.

References

Ben-Porath YS (2012). *Interpreting the MMPI-2-RF*. Minneapolis, MN: University of Minnesota Press.

Bigler ED (2015). *Use of Symptom Validity Tests and Performance Validity Tests in Disability Determinations*. Washington, DC: The Institute of Medicine.

Centers for Disease Control and Prevention (2015). *US Public Health Service Syphilis Study at Tuskegee*. [Online.] Centers for Disease Control and Prevention. www.cdc.gov/tuskegee/timeline.htm (accessed 13 December 2018).

Hathaway SR, McKinley JC (1943). *The Minnesota multiphasic personality inventory* (revised ed.). Minneapolis, MN: University of Minnesota Press.

McLuhan M (1964). *Understanding Media: the extensions of man*. New York, NY: McGraw-Hill.

Morey LC (2007). *Personality Assessment Inventory (PAI): professional manual* (2nd ed). Lutz, FL: Psychological Assessment Resources Inc.

Murakami H (2001). *Sputnik Sweetheart*. New York, NY: Vintage International.

7

The delusion of a shared language

Were you thinking that those were the words –
those upright lines? Those curves, angles, dots?
No, those are not the words – the substantial words
are in the ground and sea,
They are in the air – they are in you.
Walt Whitman (1867: 215)

If you are reading these words, taking them in and mulling them over, or perhaps not fully paying attention, you are human. We have a lot in common. But the personal meaning of the words we use is not one of them. I'm writing this in English, with the understanding that you will misunderstand me, and the hope that nevertheless you will find relevant personal truths. The meanings we find and hold in words are unique to each of us. These meanings live and continually morph within each of us, based on a lifetime of vast experiences that gives context and colour to each word we use. The meanings we each have for the words we use with each other are generally close enough that we often think they are the same. When we have this tacit agreement about shared meanings of words, it may even seem we are sharing the same experiences. When we believe this, we are fools. Words and sentences are theories that point to something beyond them. They seem like real things, or at least look like something we can all agree is the same, but even then they break down. Only real things are real things. Our understanding of words and the real things they point to is unique to each of us, with a reality that changes with experience over time.

René Magritte painted 'The Treachery of Images' in 1929 – a simple image of a pipe floating above the words, 'Ceci n'est pas une pipe'. And, of course, it is not a pipe; it is an image of a pipe. Taking this further, the word 'pipe' is not a pipe; it is just a word we use to communicate about the idea or the object. We have enough agreement about the word to use it in our language and communication but, at the same time, each of us holds our own context that imbues this word with individual meaning. And it is at that level, the level of the individual with a unique history of associations with the word, that communication often fails us. It is at this level that language can fall short.

Words distract us from individual realities, including our own. Words create unexamined and unchallenged realities, separate from individual experiences, that can lead to illusion and misunderstanding. They easily can lead us astray. This is not a novel idea. The Jewish sage Avtalyon, who lived a century before the Romans destroyed the Second Temple in Jerusalem in the year 70 of the Common Era, is credited with saying:

> Be careful with words. C-O-W gives no milk. M-A-N-U-R-E has no stench. L-O-V-E knows no passion. Mistake words for truth and you exile yourself from reality. (Shapiro, 1993: 12)

Once words are strung together, they carry our thoughts with them and carry us away all the more rapidly from real things, from ourselves and from each other. Our thoughts take over and we don't recognise that the distance between us and reality has grown, making it easier not to think about questioning the words themselves. Words offer a compelling and seductive focus for the mind. Centuries before Avtalyon, elsewhere on the massive Asian continent, the Chinese sage Lao Tzu observed: 'A mind filled with thought, identified with its own perceptions, beholds the mere forms of this world' (2001: 14). Words and the languages built with them are the ultimate in unexamined theory. When we use them, without questioning our different understanding of their meanings, we are engaging in a game of make-believe.

We are social beings. As social beings, language is one of our most important tools for connecting with each other. While we each have a unique reality, perception and experience of the world, language flattens those unique experiences by presenting a shared set of symbols and signs in infinite combinations that theoretically represent shared understandings that do not actually exist at the individual level. Dictionaries ensure that this broad falsehood of shared experience is codified. They give words the appearance of truth, a truth we assume we all share because we all know their definitions or can look up their definitions in the same place. Yet the definitions, even if agreed upon, cannot possibly reflect the unique set of experiences each of us associates with a word that colours it for us and gives it personal meaning.

Words hold as many meanings as there are people using them. In this sense – our agreement that we share the same meanings – words may be the first conspiracy of our existence as social beings. We all unwittingly play a role. We are co-conspirators in keeping each other's reality at a distance by sharing language without questioning what exists beyond the words, and without questioning the different understandings we each hold. Some people use words in ways that are so beguiling we don't realise they may be spinning conspiracies with them, layered over the ultimate conspiracy of words that already distances us from reality. And we mistake their words for truth, convinced we have heard and understood reality. I don't mean this in a paranoid way, although I suppose, given the power of words and what they can invoke, I should have steered clear of using the word 'conspiracy'. But when I reflect on its etymology, I think I am using it correctly, perhaps in the original sense, if not the popular one. These are the Latin roots of the word 'conspire': to breathe with or breathe together. Conspire – its roots reveal it to be a beautiful word, but a word that nonetheless hides a potential cost behind the beauty of the dream of unity. Breathing together suggests something positive and beautiful, rather than something sinister. Words allow me to write my thoughts and share them with you. They allow you to read them and have your own thoughts, and perhaps even feel some kind of connection with me in the process. This may occur even after these words survive me. These words, now that they are in print, also take on a life or trajectory of their own, while my own thinking may shift or become more nuanced. Even so, words allow us to engage as social beings, to live, love, laugh and learn together. They also allow us to lie together, though we may not be aware we are complicit in a lie.

This is the hidden cost of our conspiracy, the cost of not paying attention, of tuning out and assuming we mean the same thing, thereby losing the other person who is trying to communicate something unique to us. Appreciating and understanding individuality does not have to be sacrificed, but it is all too easy to do. Through our words and language, we breathe together. The illusion that we see things the same way because we seem to be breathing as one, through what appear to be shared meanings, is powerful. Ironically, breathing together through language can hide us from each other. It is a sort of Catch 22. What serves to bring us together can also keep us apart. It is a true conspiracy, yet we rely on it as our most common way of connecting with each other. And while my experiences tell me all is one, that all things are part of the larger space–time fabric as it continually unfolds, that does not mean individuality should be valued less than oneness and rendered meaningless. The unique and the universal both have value and importance, but unquestioned words favour the universal at the expense of the individual.

Words and the way our languages are structured shape us. They influence how we think and how we experience and understand ourselves, others and the world. They are a powerful force that guides how we listen and what we listen for. Anyone who speaks more than one language may recognise this when they reflect on their own experiences. If you speak only one language, I encourage you to learn another. I see the world differently when I speak, hear, read, write or sing in another language. I express myself differently when I speak another language. I feel different. Translation can never fully capture this difference, and important nuances of meaning and experience are lost. I love reading Federico Garcia Lorca and Pablo Neruda in the original Spanish and have never found a satisfying translation that gives me the same experience of their poetry in English. I am certain I am missing a great deal when I read novels in English by Natsume Soseki, Yukio Mishima and Haruki Murakami. When people who are multilingual speak English, cultural meanings embedded in their words may be lost on us. Speaking the same language does not mean we carry the same cultural experiences that shape our meanings.

If you speak only English, it is a mistake to assume that a multilingual person speaking English means what you do when you speak the same words. Tagalog, a language spoken in the Philippines, offers powerful examples. Tagalog includes words from Spanish and English, the languages of two colonial powers that occupied the Philippines over a period of almost 400 years. However, the words from those languages sometimes hold different meanings in Tagalog. In Tagalog, the word for 'maybe' is the same as the word used for 'sure' in Spanish: *siguro* (spelled *seguro* in Spanish). To say 'sure' in Tagalog, the word *sigurado* (spelled *asegurado* in Spanish) is used. *Asegurado* means 'sure' or 'assured' in Spanish. This is not an accident of translation from Spanish to Tagalog. There is culture embedded in these words and how they are used that reflects an important value in the Philippines of helping others to save face. Rather than say 'no' to you, Filipinos may be more likely to say 'maybe'. This face-saving 'maybe' is carried through a word that means 'sure' in Spanish, rather than the Spanish word for 'maybe' (*tal vez*). In other words, maybe can mean no, and the use of the Spanish word 'seguro' (sure) smooths over this intent. This cultural meaning may also carry over when Filipinos say 'maybe' in English, and you may not realise that you actually have been told 'no'. The Tagalog use of *siguro* may also reflect a subtle act of defiance in the face of Spanish oppression: saying 'sure' in the coloniser's language, but actually meaning 'no'.

Even the absence of words can have a different meaning, and this can be lost in a cross-cultural translation. For example, in Filipino culture, when someone is angry and silent, this may be to save face for you rather than embarrass you with their anger. There is even a word for it in Tagalog: *tampo*. Speaking more than one language can allow for a perspective that appreciates the conspiracy of words hiding individual meanings that each of us holds.

When we encounter a translation, we accept that our understanding falls short of what must have been expressed. Yet when we speak the same language, we don't think about what might have been lost in our understanding. When we speak the same language, we assume we don't need a translator. We are wrong. Your words capture your experience in a way I will never actually know. To understand you better, I will probably have to ask you to translate for me, to explain to me what your words mean to you. There are more than seven billion languages spoken in the world. Among these, we may speak the same language, but we don't share it. We may use the same words, but our personal experiences that are tied to the same words are not the same. If I insist on understanding your words through my own meanings, I have lost you, because my ability to translate is deficient.

The more we talk about other people with words that we fool ourselves into believing are universal, the more we keep ourselves from seeing other people as individuals. We cannot trust our own meanings for words to figure out what someone means by the words they use. Each person's language, the words they use and how they use them, carries the intersection of the manifold sources of their unique identity. It is a true reflection of diversity if we take the time to listen carefully. This is the ultimate challenge in empathic understanding. It is also one of the ultimate challenges in truly appreciating and respecting diversity. The challenge in part is to be aware of what gets in the way of hearing the other person and accepting and valuing their individual reality as truly different – to accept the meanings they give us in the words they use.

As psychologists, it does not matter whether we do therapy or assessment, people use words to communicate their unique experiences to us. We may also give them psychological tests, with words chosen by someone else for them to answer. Indeed, a person I worked with once shared with me his reaction to a psychological test I had given him in the format of a multiple-choice questionnaire: 'That thing, I don't see it as a questionnaire, I see it as like their choices. So, which one do you choose? It's not my choices, it's not what I feel.' It might be of value to reflect on whether we impose our meanings for words on other people or allow other people to choose their own words with their own meanings to define themselves.

We build elaborate theories out of words: theories of personality, theories of psychopathology and diagnosis, theories of test construction and theories of individuals who face us in treatment and assessment. We use our own words with our own meanings and words borrowed from agreed-upon theories and diagnostic frameworks. Using these words encourages us to make assumptions and think in generalisations. When we think in categories, we think less about individual meanings. We hear other people's words, but we miss their meanings. Perhaps we don't even believe their meanings over our own.

The words we hear can cover over what is really being communicated when we only listen by imposing the meanings we know.

What is being communicated can be obscured further by the stereotypes we hold and what we want or need to hear. Beyond the traps of our own meanings and the filters of our stereotypes and personal issues lie the structures of our language itself. Every language shapes the user's reality by the words it includes, and by the words that are absent. Although a shift may be occurring, English has long been a language dominated by the dualist classification of gender as female or male. Tagalog, by contrast, often makes use of a non-gendered word, *siya*, to talk about a person, regardless of their gender or gender identity. I should add that *siya* does not mean 'it'; rather, it truly signifies another person in a genderless way. This simple difference may shape the way English and Tagalog speakers think about and see the world, and how they hear each other. Our languages set up categories, or boxes, for our thinking, and our thoughts are easily and rapidly dropped into those boxes. Our languages shape our thoughts and what we are likely to hear from another person. Our willingness to add words to our language and our knowledge of words in other languages can determine how open we are to possible meanings that lie beyond the comfortable and familiar.

As psychologists, we are often faced with two roads that diverge in the woods. When a person comes to us in distress, we can either impose our meaning on their words or we can be subversive. We can break free from the conspiracy of language simply by asking people what their words mean to them and by learning the words that people prefer to use to define their experiences. This second road, the road not often taken, is the road of radical empathy described by Carl Rogers: the path of prizing other people and their unique realities enough not to define them by our own reality and to listen carefully and thoughtfully to how they define themselves. Can we let people be their own dictionaries?

In an earlier thought-piece on non-directivity as a foundational attitude in client-centred work, I quoted a passage from *Sylvie and Bruno Concluded*, by Lewis Carroll (1893), which offers another metaphor that is also relevant here:

'That's another thing we've learned from your Nation,' said Mein Herr, 'map-making. But we've carried it much further than you.

What do you consider the largest map that would be really useful?'

'About six inches to the mile.'

'Only six inches!' exclaimed Mein Herr. 'We very soon got to six yards to the mile. Then we tried a hundred yards to the mile. And then came the grandest idea of all! We actually made a map of the country on the scale of a mile to the mile!'

'Have you used it much?' I enquired.

'It has never been spread out, yet,' said Mein Herr: 'The farmers objected: they said it would cover the whole country and shut out the sunlight! So, we now use the country itself, as its own map, and I assure you it does nearly as well.'

The people we see in our work are actively making their own maps. Are we able to let them guide us through the maps they are making when they express themselves to us, or do we need to impose our own map or our understanding of their map from our perspective? Can we overcome our fears and our need for power that are expressed through our control over how another person's reality is defined? Can we risk putting down our own maps long enough to learn a new world? Can we allow ourselves to be the stranger in a strange land? It may seem like an odd suggestion, but when we see people in the work that we do, perhaps it is more powerful to see ourselves as the stranger. How might we encounter the other person's words and expressions if we accepted this perspective?

How we face another person's words, how we encounter their words, says a lot about our comfort with letting go of power over others. The words another person chooses to give us can also say a lot about how safe they feel with us. The words we use with each other determine how close we let each other get. The words you use as a psychologist when you say you are trying to understand me may inform whether I believe that is the case. Will I be comfortable with the words you have chosen? Do your words match your demeanour, your body language and the colour and tone of your voice? I am watching you for signs that help me determine how safe you are and how much I can trust you with my words. Do your words appear to change the reality I am expressing in ways that I do not intend and that sit uncomfortably with me? Do your words make me uncomfortable enough to shut you out by limiting or cutting off my own words? Do I simply maintain a surface discourse with you, while protecting my inner experience from you until I can leave? You have a theory of me that you are forming in your own words. Do I feel powerless in the face of the theory you are imposing? Do I let you impose your language on me and control me within the confines of your own theory? After all, you are the doctor and I am just a patient. And do you recognise this is happening? Our love of words, especially our self-centred love of our understanding of the words we all may use, is where we are likely to encounter problems. Can we break free from our love for our own meanings to listen to another person's meanings and hear their theories of themselves in their own words?

Words when used as a way to try to understand someone else are deceptively clear but typically misleading. I do my best to turn off language. This may sound odd at first, but as psychologists we may engage in an effort to gather information about what is happening with the people we see in our work through direct observation. Psychiatrists have named this exercise the 'mental status examination', which in large part includes a number of behavioural observations. People tell us things with words, and we also watch for many things beyond those words. We reflect on the quality of the other person's speech with respect to such things as volume, pressure and pace. We reflect on how extensive their vocabulary appears to be, and whether they speak English fluently or with an accent or non-standard word usage and grammatical structure. We observe whether they understand why they are seeing us, and if they know where they are and who they are. We may observe how their mood appears, and how much their mood changes in relation to what they are expressing. They may appear confused or lucid and speak in tangential or roundabout ways. We may also reflect on the general themes people are expressing and if they are highly focused on one or more themes.

We often have reactions to the person sitting in front of us, and these may elicit feelings in us, including agitation, happiness, boredom and exhaustion. This, too, is meaningful information. Even so, when we write about our observations, we do so with our words, or perhaps we borrow professional jargon. And we call these observations objective, in that they are what we observe about the other person from our perspective, not what they tell us from their subjective frame. Interestingly, we do not acknowledge the subjective bias in our objective observations. Nor do we seem to recognise the value in attempting to accurately understand and convey the other person's subjective experience.

I am reminded of one of my favourite YouTube channels, *Rachel and Jun*. The description of their channel reads: 'We're a Japanese/American married couple! We make videos about Japan and our lives!' Their show often chronicles their relationship and their cultural misunderstandings of each other, typically in a lighthearted way that captures the love they have for each other. I find them a lot of fun to watch. In one clip, 'What we argue about | Japanese/American marriage' (2017), Rachel is talking about her struggles with how Jun apologises, saying that he doesn't show enough emotion. Jun disagrees and so she asks him to show viewers how he apologises. He looks at Rachel, who is holding the camera, and says, '*Gomenasai*'. This translates flatly as, 'I am sorry'. My experience of him is that he looks contrite and also vulnerable, but Rachel sees him from her cultural perspective and experiences him as not expressing enough feeling in his apology. If she were writing up her behavioural observations of Jun, based on conducting a mental status examination, she might even say that Jun has blunted or flat affect. This would clearly be from her perspective. As an objective observation, using her words and cultural perspective would miss what appears to be a quite sincere apology that certainly carries emotion. Our observations of wordless behaviours can thus carry the same biases as our understanding of the words other people use.

Some of my deepest appreciation and understanding of people who sit across from me is wordless. In this regard, I find listening to classical music reinforces my ability to get away from words and sit more directly with my experience. Music is a temporal art form. It reveals itself wordlessly over time. Great musicians recognise time as an integral aspect of their art, either instinctively or consciously. Those who are able to grasp this essential aspect of music and express it in their performances are able to help us break out of our own timeframes and enter the temporal worlds they create. This experience may help us to reconnect with parts of our experience we neglect, and it may also be healing. It certainly can be meditative, and one of the reasons I listen to classical music is to let go and follow the flow of the music in the moment as it unfolds over time, out of my control. This experience informs my attempts to understand other people beyond their words and to follow them wherever they go, as their worlds unfold over time.

Listening to classical music is a wonderful, indescribable, wordless experience. Indeed, once I put words to the experience and try to describe what I hear in a performance, the experience loses its fullness and slips away. Beethoven's last piano sonata, for me, is the expression of a great composer coming to terms with the unthinkable loss of his hearing. It sounds to me like a life review, conveying the enormity of becoming a deaf composer, recalling his once youthful vigour and sense of invulnerability, the onset of his struggles and despair, his horrible sense of loss and the eventual awareness that he can 'hear' an even more extraordinary world in his mind now that he can no longer hear the world outside of him. The music carries within it a transformation, a sense of transcendence, and a transfiguration that leads to a new musical language and awareness, a new palette, that results in heavenly wonder. Liszt's 'Vallee d'Obermann', with its poignant expression of depression and alienation from a world of beauty, is juxtaposed in my mind with his 'Dante Sonata', an expression of the utmost despair, made all the more painful by the fleeting awareness of joy that is forever and completely out of reach. The night atmosphere of Chopin's nocturnes, the gossip and street sounds in a Mozart sonata, once I begin to describe these things, the magic disappears, and whole wondrous worlds are flattened. And so, like music, once I put words to another person's experiences, how quickly they slip away and become less full in my understanding, more distant from who the other person is.

I see endless musical compositions in other people's expressions, with continually unfolding melodies and themes. And while music is supposed to be a universal language, if we both listen to a performance of a Mozart piano sonata, do we truly hear the same piece? Being married to a classical pianist, I have heard countless performances by various artists of the same piece, and I am always amazed at the differences in interpretation of the same notes, the same score. Of course, a casual listener might hear all of these performances as the same. And this may also be true of how we listen to people's words and how we come to understand their meanings. Words and musical notation hide similar conspiracies. The notes on a score are always pointing to something beyond them that is or was in someone else's mind. Musicians, in a sense, look at the notes on a page, in the context of a score, and attempt to have conversations with composers, who are typically no longer alive. What was in the composer's head? How was the composer's reality impacted by their era and the context of their own experiences? Unless the composer is alive, to interact with and get feedback from, the meaning locked in the notes is highly educated guesswork.

To a great extent, the artist's conceptualisation can never be confirmed, although a great performance will carry with it an air of truth and genuineness. Different artists will interpret and understand the same set of notes in a score differently. An artist's fidelity to the score, to the exact notations on the page, can be so rigid that they miss what is there beyond the notes. In these instances, a machine might play the piece just as convincingly. In other instances, artists may impose their own vision in a way that is uniquely compelling but leaves the composer unrecognisable. I often think of the unimaginable task that musicians have, trying to make sense of black dots on a page that point to something far more meaningful, rich and complex that lies beyond them in the imaginings of a person who likely is now long dead.

Psychologists are lucky. The people we are trying to understand are sitting right in front of us. We are not having conversations with dead people, and we can actually check in with them: 'Is this what you meant?' or, 'I don't think I understand, what do you mean by that?' When we listen to other people, can we hear more than the words we think we know? Can we pay attention to their broader context and to their flow as they unfold? Can we hear the subtleties in a person's voice, their choice of words, motifs and conflicting themes? Can we hear what is not said, the silences, what exists between the notes? Can we hear their words and sentences over time, taking care not to miss the greater meaning embedded in their spoken words by holding rigidly to what we think a word should mean? Can we keep from getting caught up in imposing our own reality? Every person's words are a work of art, a unique expression pregnant with meaning. The question for us as psychologists is whether we are willing to be music lovers.

References

Carroll L (1893). *Sylvie and Bruno Concluded*. London: Macmillan & Co.

Lao Tzu (2001). *Tao Te Ching: the definitive edition* (Star J, trans). New York, NY: Jeremy P Tarcher/Penguin.

Rachel and Jun (2017). *What we argue about: Japanese/American marriage*. [Video.] YouTube. www.youtube.com/watch?v=V0reQCDL968 (accessed 17 November 2018).

Shapiro RM (1993). *Wisdom of the Sages: a modern reading of Pirke Avot*. New York, NY: Bell Tower.

Whitman W (1867). To the sayers of words. In: Whitman W. *Leaves of Grass*. New York, NY: WE Chapin & Co.

Part 3

The impersonal
is political

8

Welcome to the machine

I don't think anyone has seen the real Frank Zappa because being
interviewed is one of the most abnormal things you can do to
somebody else. It's two steps removed from the inquisition.
Frank Zappa (Schutte, 2016)

Our work with people is filled with opportunities to dehumanise them
and ourselves. We often are not likely to recognise these opportunities,
which are rather abundant. When we do have moments of recognition,
we may be motivated on some level to pretend it is not happening,
that we are not taking part in something that harms people, and that
it has no impact on us. Unfortunately, the interplay of our profession
with the systems within which we find ourselves working reinforces
these opportunities, keeping us from the fullness of an encounter with
another person.

Systems, in many ways, embody the people who create them, but of
course not in a literal, living body. It seems fairly obvious that systems
are not people. However, given the Supreme Court of the United States
(SCOTUS) decision *Burwell v Hobby Lobby Stores, Inc* (2014), which
expanded the rights of corporations to be treated like people, perhaps
it is not so obvious to everyone. Despite the SCOTUS decision,
corporations really are not people, and neither are systems. Systems,
like corporations, may reflect the thoughts, emotions and intentions of
people, as well as the power held and expressed by those who created

them. But they are not people. Systems are impersonal. When we enter them, we risk losing our own personhood and depersonalising other people. In depersonalising other people, or agreeing to their depersonalisation, we depersonalise ourselves. We shrink and deaden our humanity little by little, and somehow don't recognise this is what we are doing to ourselves and others. It is a phenomenal state of denial we share in and that is reinforced by the systems we work within and that shape our daily lives. Yet many of us still choose to enter systems and work within them, some of us knowing what we will face and others not recognising what we are entering.

The people we encounter in our work typically have no better alternative, and in some systems have no choice, and so they join us there. A person attending our clinic for an assessment was aware of our advocacy efforts to educate the government about the impact of legislation on people accessing mental health services. When he presented for his intake appointment with my friend and business partner, he was also aware that she is Jewish. Aside from her name, it is hard to miss the ancient coin hanging from her necklace, set in a star of David. This man expressed a great deal of anger about the auto insurance system, through which he was seeking assistance, and told her, 'and you are driving the train to Auschwitz!' Aside from being provocative, his statement nonetheless captures something essential about the impersonal and dehumanising nature of systems and the harm that they can bring about. It also speaks to the reality that, even if we have good intentions, we have chosen to work within a system that people experience as harmful, and perhaps even lethal.

We cannot help but be compromised to some extent by the systems we work within. If we work within a system long enough, we may even stop recognising the system and how it has been changing us. At the risk of sounding paranoid, systems carry within them conspiracies so big they do not need to be covered up. Systems become like the air we breathe. Whether we enter a system to work or we attempt to work outside of systems, there are always powers and influences to face and acknowledge, to come to terms with, in order to do our work as honestly as possible. We may work in a system to make money, to make a difference or because we believe in the system. The question becomes how aware we are of who or what we serve, what role or roles we may be playing in this service, and how our goals are shaped in relation to the people we encounter in our work.

The system enshrines a power dynamic. Roles and goals are explicitly laid out. They are defined by the system, and then further defined by each of us when we take them on. They become masks we may not realise we are wearing; filters we may not realise we are using. Our roles and goals then shape our actions, and our actions reinforce our roles and goals. Our own issues also move us towards roles and goals that reinforce what we need and determine how strongly we will adhere to our roles. The system also reinforces our needs and unacknowledged issues. Because of this, it is not surprising that we might be blind to the harms it reinforces.

Systems offer us a variety of roles. Here I offer only a scant exploration of a phenomenon that surely could fill volumes. Doctor is a role many of my friends and I fill. It can feel good to be called doctor, or the friendlier 'doc', to be seen as educated, knowledgeable and powerful in some way. To hold authority. To be an authority. To be authority. As psychologists, we are often insecure about being doctors, about recognising ourselves as doctors, while also wanting people to know we are doctors. Holding this identity carries the risk of making us rigid and defensive, and this risk can make us likely to shut down any challenges to our authority. Yet these challenges might actually be important avenues of expression for the people we encounter.

The expert role is closely related, with a similar promise of reinforcing our sense of power and self-worth. It also holds similar potential for distracting us from more closely seeing the people we work with in various ways. Being an expert, it is easy to become self-absorbed and lose our humility, which is an essential orientation to the world that maintains our humanity, our capacity to be genuine and real. Scientist is another tempting role, as many of us are trained in science, to a lesser or greater degree. Of course, science has its traps, as I have described already, and taking on the role of scientist brings us in closer proximity to the traps inherent in this belief system and its method when adhered to without question. It also reinforces the primacy of objective information. The objective is prized over the subjective to the extent that subjectivity is often ridiculed as a source of information. The more we hold fast to the role of scientist, the more we may be convinced that we should only follow objective data, and the more we may be vulnerable to objectifying people.

Alongside these roles, many of us hope to be seen at least as professionals. We try to comport ourselves as professionals, and we may aspire to be the consummate professional. And what exactly does this mean? Are there ways we lose ourselves to this role, also? What does it mean to be unprofessional? How frightened are we that we will be seen in this way – perhaps labelled by our colleagues or bosses in the system? When this happens, we may end up watching our own actions to the point of stifling our best instincts, our creativity, and what is genuine in us.

Perhaps the most concerning roles are lie detector and saviour. Each holds great power in terms of shoring up our sense of being good people. At the same time, each holds great power in keeping us from seeing the individual people we work with more fully for who they are. To be a saviour, someone has to be saved – but they may not actually need saving, or could very well save themselves. We often try to save people by defining the saving they need, and by making the assumption or holding the surety that they need saving and we are the ones to do it. It is an easy way to feel powerful and to feel good. Our perception that people need to be saved reinforces our perception of them as powerless, and we may set out on an ill-conceived journey, causing harms we are unaware of. In taking on this role, we can miss the power the other person has to help themselves and actively undermine them.

If we take on the saviour role, we are essentially caring about ourselves first. We tell ourselves we are doing it to help, we are doing it to give someone a better life, we are doing it to change someone for the better. It can feel good, but we are still caring too much about ourselves, and our role both hides this and reinforces our good feelings about ourselves.

Being a lie detector is also a way of being a saviour – a saviour of the system we work within, or a society that we live in. If we are lie detectors, the main goal will be uncovering deception and we may come to see deception where it does not exist. Enough information may come together to support a view that the other person is deceiving us, and then it is hard to see beyond this to the complexities and nuances that might paint another story that is closer to the truth. The gatekeeper role is a hybrid of the expert and the lie detector. The gatekeeper determines who has access to the system, who can pass by to get services. Of course, not everyone is truthful. It is a difficult question to address when we consider where we stand in relation to that awareness without being naive and without being so hardened that we see everyone as lying. Just as everyone is not truthful, not everyone is lying. We can see someone as impaired when they are not, but we can also miss a person's real distress by looking for them to be dishonest.

Whether we realise it or not, we get something out of playing a role. Roles provide comfort, a certain familiarity and regularity that can ease anxiety born of uncertainties and fears, a persona that will be readily accepted by the people we face in our work, as well as by colleagues and others. When we identify with or blindly adhere to roles, it is likely that we will care too much about ourselves when we encounter other people. We become our roles. They allow us to feel like we are good people and help shield us from having to open our eyes fully to painful truths that are present in the room. Roles blind us and are also filters that set us up to judge. They bias us and limit our possibilities for seeing clearly and listening cleanly. As someone I worked with once shared with me: 'Everybody tries to make me out the way they want to and not the way it is.' The roles we adhere to may also keep us from recognising harms we may be doing. Recognising and reminding ourselves of this are essential and ongoing tasks if we care to understand and appreciate others more fully for who they are. Awareness is the key to loosening the grip that roles have on us, freeing us to be more genuine in the moment and more likely to understand the person in front of us.

Goals flow from roles. If we are the experts, the authorities, who better to set the goals, to define and measure them? If we are saviours or lie detectors, the goals remain ours in relation to what we hear, how we define help and who needs it. If we are scientists, our goals become tied to our research studies. Goals are also defined, structured and limited by the system within which we work. All of this is likely to be at odds with the goals that people have when they come to see us in our offices. Some clinicians may come to see the question of whose goals we are addressing as murky. In other words, who exactly is the client? Being raised client-centred, I grew up professionally using the term 'client' for the people I face directly in my work. The notion implies an awareness of the power and rights of the people we work with to self-direct. It is a stance of giving up power over others.

How we see our role will shape our perception of who our clients are. Better still, to my mind, is simply to see the people I face in my work as people. Who the 'client' is may not be agreed upon in the systems within which we work, but the stance we take towards this question influences our goals, which will necessarily shape the nature and quality of our interactions with the people we encounter in our work and how we hear them. The answer to who the client is may seem obvious but working within systems makes the issue complex. In fact, there are likely to be multiple answers, all of which are true in some way. For example, in my work doing legal assessments, I get referrals from lawyers seeking answers to their questions, I assess the people they are asking questions about, and I have an obligation to judges, arbitrators and juries when I testify. If I must use the word 'client', they are all clients. I see myself as responsible to all of these people, and I also try to be guided by the fundamental principle of clinical work with respect to the people I assess: to do no harm. For me, this is an ever-present goal. I try to hold this ethical obligation to the people I face in my work, regardless of my role. This goal requires me to use my expertise to understand the person I am assessing as clearly as possible, wherever that leads me, and to respect their personhood even if they are being dishonest.

Systems provide parameters for those who operate within them, and these are often defined in terms of money and time. In order to receive funding for our work, we typically must show evidence that our work is worth funding; that we are making some sort of progress towards goals that are accepted within the system. The pressure to prove progress, to provide objective data and to move things along is inherent to funding in most systems. Money and time become linked and we may be trapped by both. We are working, after all, and most of us rely on an income to live. We are pressured to follow the clock. This situation creates obvious pressures; our work becomes driven by fear and reward, rather than by the human encounter and the hope of discovering and understanding a person for who they are. When money and time are real sources of pressure, efficiency becomes important, and it is a double-edged sword. Sometimes efficiency allows us to focus better on the parts of our work that are most essential, such as understanding the people we face. However, it can also mean spending less time with them. Saving time in the interest of making money or doing our work in less time than is reasonable, because of the constraints we face in systems, lead us towards engaging in briefer and less meaningful encounters.

We may feel more pressure directly or indirectly to do lower quality work. Perhaps the system lays out a framework for lower quality work. Perhaps a boss asks for corners to be cut, or there just is not enough time, or we do not get paid enough to do what we think is a better job. We may find ourselves concerned with earning more, or earning enough, if the system doesn't pay enough for the work. Faced by these pressures, we may find ourselves swept up in a process of systemic and systematic depersonalisation that occurs right in front of our eyes – eyes that are wide shut. The system is a potent reinforcer of the variables that keep the people we work with at arm's length, or further; a reinforcer that blinds us to the fullness of the people we encounter. Unfortunately, the more we speed up or go through the motions in our work, the more we are vulnerable to the power of systems to diminish our personhood and the personhood of the people we encounter in our work.

Systems define time constraints, and we often make up our own. Our classic made-up time constraint is the 50-minute psychotherapy hour, which we then stack up over the course of a day to do a full day's work. And then our own tendencies determine how rigidly we adhere to the constraints we make up, or the ones we believe we must follow within a system. At the same time, our time is not limitless, and we face real obstacles in this sense. Who is paying can also impact on how the time is spent. When treatment is paid for by a third party, we may find ourselves agreeing to a mandate or expectations beyond those of the person coming to see us. Within a system, there may be clear parameters with respect to how many sessions are being funded and how long those sessions can be. The time pressures built into systems encourage us to try pushing the river – that is, getting someone to progress, whatever that means, much sooner than may be natural or helpful. Few if any of us can survive doing only pro-bono work, and many of us are not able to figure out how to make a practice based solely on private pay a workable and sustainable situation. And so, we often find ourselves working within systems without the luxury of being able to ignore time. In these situations, I find the only way around this dilemma is to face it squarely and openly and be honest with the people I work with about the limitations facing both of us. This is the number of sessions we are approved for. This is how much time we have been given. These are the goals that have been approved for our time together. This is an honest starting point for facing these constraints together and determining how we go forward.

In my work doing psychological legal assessments, I have done my best to give myself every opportunity to ignore time. Ignoring time is my most powerful ally when I hope to encounter another person fully and understand them as best I can from their perspective. The more time we have, or the less pressured we feel by time, the more space there is to hear the other person, to attempt to understand them more clearly, without imposing our frame on their story and without changing their story. That is why I don't have a clock in my office and I don't wear a watch. We are all story-tellers, but we may not be able to tell our story under circumstances that limit us in various ways. Time is the most obvious limit on our ability to tell our story, and if there is not enough of it, it impacts on our comfort and trust to tell any of it. If we have a half hour to tell our story, we will tell a very different story than if we have four hours, or if we know we are not limited by time and the clinician working with us will take as long as it takes to understand us. After an hour or two, someone still may not be heard and may not be comfortable letting themselves be heard. They are well aware that we have given them limited time to tell their story. The overwhelmed person experiencing distress and wanting to be heard may appear to be exaggerating, unco-operative and inconsistent, simply because we have set them up to not be able to open up to us at a natural pace, making them feel a greater urgency to be heard.

Roles, goals, money and time – these are all powerful influences on how we encounter other people. These also influence the tools we use, including our listening skills and our psychological tests. These tools become products of the system we are working within as a result of the way systemic pressures impact on their use. They are co-opted; they are compromised. In this way, I see our tools as emissaries of the system, reflecting the system through their use. In the field of psychology, the clinical interview may be our most ubiquitous tool. If the medium is the message, and I believe it is, the interviews we carry out hold within them a reflection of the dehumanising influence the system has on us and on the people we encounter in our work.

While our relationship with people in our work begins before the interview, my view is that the interview itself cannot begin without a transparent discussion of informed consent. I believe a fully informed consent should mean something, that the person I am facing should actually be fully informed about who I am, what we are going to be doing, what they can expect of me, how I will use what they tell me, and what the implications are for them in the future. A fully informed consent also means making sure that the person I am working with understands and knows that they have the ultimate power, at any time, to walk away, and that I really am OK with that. Regardless of the context of an interview, I am working with another person in my office. We meet quite literally in my world. It is a very real reminder that I have power in the context of our interaction. It only makes sense to me to find a way to be welcoming of the stranger coming into my strange land, to be transparent and real about what I understand of what we are about to embark upon, and to be up-front and completely comfortable about the power the other person has to leave – for them to be able at any time to stop and say, 'This is not for me.'

I offer people the opportunity, always, to ask me questions. I am fine with being interrupted. I am fine with cell phones ringing and being answered. Some people who have suffered a traumatic loss, perhaps a loved one has been killed, may have a stronger need to answer phone calls immediately. I have time, I don't mind, and it also allows more of their world into my office and tells me more about what their world looks like. If I force them into my constraints, I may miss an important part of their story. I am also fine, and I always ask, if someone needs the lights dimmed because of sensitivity to light, or if they need a different chair or to lie down. There are simple things I can do to be human and to see the other person's humanity, even if we are not entering a therapy relationship, even if my job, my goal within the system, is to understand someone well enough to answer their lawyer's questions and to explain my understanding to a judge, jury or arbitrator. From my perspective, no time is ever wasted, and so I don't want to make time into a pressure or a worry and lose something by squeezing the life out of time. Sometimes just getting through a fully informed consent can take up to an hour or so. During that time, the other person and I are starting to get to know each other. The person I am interviewing is already sharing their story in direct and indirect ways as they respond to the content and the process of my going over consent.

Given the emphasis in clinical psychology on gathering objective information and the pressures within systems to move things along, bringing the other person's reality into the interview and welcoming it, giving it a place, may be the greatest challenge. The psychological method includes gathering significant sources of objective information that we call data, such as objective psychological test scores. Even behavioural observations and information gathered from file reviews may be considered a form of objective information. The psychiatric method considers behavioural observations to be objective, which perhaps says a great deal about whose reality is paramount: your reality is subjective, and I call my observation of your reality objective, even though it reflects my subjective reality as I observe you. If we acknowledge the subjective as meaningful, since the interview has a place in the psychological method, surely we would want to find a way to understand the other person's subjectivity, the other person's reality and experience, as best we can, and minimise our influence on it from our own countless biases? We would understand that objectifying someone's reality changes it. When we objectify the other person's reality, we make it an object for our examination, curating a reality to fill our own personal museum. If we value the subjective then we would want to encounter the subjective in other people as fully and honestly as possible, without altering it, without shrinking it, without bending it to our reality or some other reality defined by others.

When I carry out a psychological legal assessment, I always bring the testing people have engaged in earlier into the interview, in an effort to humanise the data. I also encourage this practice when clinicians carry out assessments as a part of their treatment work in our clinic. In Chapter 6, I explored the human side of the numbers and the power of the numbers to obscure a person's experience. I find it helpful to review the test data, the numbers, before I go further in the interview process, and I ask questions in order to hear how the person I am facing understood the test items when they responded to them. In the short time that this takes, important, living context becomes clear that otherwise would be hidden by the lifeless numbers.

Time constraints, reinforced by the profit motive, may also encourage us to use more brief psychological tests as part of an assessment. Brief tests, such as brief symptom surveys, may make sense when they are used to track progress across treatment. However, in the assessment context, brief surveys can lead us to miss things, just as brief interviews and brief therapy sessions under time constraint can lead us to miss things. People who tend to hold back will do just that in response to a brief survey. A longer questionnaire that includes measures to understand a person's response style or tendency may let us know that someone is likely to be holding back and may not be as happy and healthy as they initially seem, especially if we don't take enough time to see them when we face them in our work. A common game I see played between assessors and the people they are assessing is akin to, 'Let's get through this quickly so neither of us has to end up being uncomfortable with the bad things that may be going on. It will all be over soon and we can both go home without any of the mess.'

If test scores suggest a person tends to minimise or downplay their distress, I want to learn more about that during the interview. I want to know if that is happening in the interview and if I need to change how I ask questions in order to make sure I hear the other person's story. There are many reasons a person might hold back: culture; not trusting that other people will hear them; a need to fool themselves; the need to see themselves as fine or for others to see them as fine; an inability to access their experience quickly and put words to it readily if it is painful to do so – the list goes on. One person told me, 'Some questions I don't really want to talk about because I don't want to talk about my emotions. Like after this accident I was a different person completely. I was active, working, playing baseball; the accident happened. [Now] everything annoys me, friends annoy me. I want to keep it inside of me.'

Another fairly typical explanation goes as follows: 'I don't talk about things or say things because then I have to face that things are going downhill, and I don't know how to face them.' Another person who felt particularly vulnerable explained that she needed me to think she was not vulnerable, 'probably because I didn't want to portray myself in danger. Like when I go out anywhere, sometimes I double up on my pain medications so I can go out, and wear things over my sling so I don't look vulnerable, and don't put myself in danger that way, so I don't look weak. Sorry.' She apologised for being tearful, her face was red, and she blew her nose before continuing: 'I live by myself, so I don't want to be vulnerable, I have to take care of myself all the time. And I try to stay as strong and as healthy as I can, but it doesn't always work.'

It may be shocking, but it turns out that many people do not want to share the depth of their suffering with a total stranger in an unfamiliar place. And if we don't think to ask after reflecting on data we have right in front of us, many people are happy to hide it and get the interview over with. It is a nice little dance. We keep each other from bringing pain into the room. Perhaps the person we interview is not the only one who doesn't want to face it. Our roles, goals, money and time may help us with our avoidance, making the system an easier place for us to work.

If the way a person responded to test items doesn't make sense to me, I don't have to guess. I can ask that person directly during the interview: 'You answered that you eat rocks for dinner. What did you mean by that?' It is straightforward and simple, but it takes time and also means recognising the person in front of us as a source of information beyond the numbers. I also want to know the person's experience during testing. Did they need to take more medication than usual before or while filling out the questionnaires or engaging in tests of cognitive functioning? Why did they ask for the tests to be read to them rather than reading themselves? Are they unable to read? Do they have difficulties understanding English? Do they have visual difficulties that prevent them from reading? Do they have problems with fine motor skills, requiring someone else to fill in the questionnaires under their direction? Did they have increasing distress or pain over the course of testing and afterwards, and what impact did this have?

Asking about a person's experience with the tests shows that we understand there is more to it than just numbers and that we want to understand them better. It communicates interest in them and respect for the effort they took to engage in tests that may have been difficult for them. It also communicates early on that we are comfortable with discussing potentially difficult emotional issues. 'You responded to many items indicating that life has no meaning to you and you would rather be dead, can you tell me more about that?' 'You noted that drinking is a problem for you – in what way is it a problem for you?' 'You noted that sometimes you completely lose control of your temper, how does that look?' I am curious about what the other person is communicating about their life. I want to use the interview to understand the person beyond the numbers and the details in their file, by facing them as fully as I can.

The file – the collection of previous reports and records – can also suck the humanity out of an interview and skew our understanding of the person we are facing, especially when we use it to challenge them or when we allow our conclusions to be influenced by those already made by other people. Yet how we use the file doesn't have to further dehumanise the interview process. I want to be able to understand incomplete information and potential inconsistencies that I come across in the file, but grilling someone is not the best way to reach that understanding. We can bring the file into the interview transparently, and reflect on it and the obvious questions it may hold for us. It may sometimes be difficult to keep from jumping to conclusions after reading a slew of seemingly convincing reports about what is happening with someone, but it's essential to hold off. Otherwise, why carry out the interview if it is just to confirm what everyone else has written? I might as well write a summary of all those other conclusions and sign my name to it – no more need to see people. Sometimes people are not sure what their family physician means by something they have written, or they may not understand a code entered on a billing summary. It often makes sense, eventually, if I carefully follow the person I am interviewing and I don't worry about the time. To assume what appears obvious – that the person I am seeing must be lying – is not always right. Unfortunately, if we are rushed to judgement and rushed to finish, this is often the only answer we can see.

The longest assessment interview I have been a part of was about eight hours, broken into two sessions. The person I was interviewing wanted to keep going after four hours, but I needed to stop. Having first explained informed consent, I brought the contents of their file into our discussion. It was sitting in the room with us, several banker's boxes of paper sorted into legal binders. I told her, very simply: 'When I read the file, everyone seems to come to the conclusion that you are lying.' She looked at me, barely able to contain her emotion, and said in a loud and pressured voice: 'I know! And I don't know why!' I let her know that I didn't either, since we had just met, but that I wanted to spend as much time as necessary to figure that out. I had no idea what I was in for, and certainly did not expect eight hours of interviewing.

What unfolded was a story of the most horrific, lifelong abuse, beginning in childhood, when she was abused and then abandoned by her parents, then passed from foster home to foster home, and later imprisoned by her father in his basement and forced to bear his children. The layers of trauma and distress were unimaginable. As humans, we really do this to each other. The realities I learn about are always beyond what I could imagine on my own. And this woman somehow survived all of this and was sitting in front of me. None of this story was to be found in the many files sitting on the desk – at least not in a human, fleshed out, real way. The reports were replete with stories of how over the top and exaggerated her presentation was, how tangential she was, how inconsistent she was with remembering details, and even how unco-operative she was when faced with a panel of interviewers who challenged her whenever she had a hard time remembering a detail accurately, leading her to be more over the top and tangential. Imagine being a woman with a lifelong history of being controlled, imprisoned and abused. How might you experience an interview with a panel that has the power to determine what happens to you?

The file may also hold more subtle questions. They may not always hold stories of exaggeration and lies explained by doctors and other health professionals. In some files we find stories in which a person seems to be doing fairly well. It might then be easy to hear a person relate, for example, a horrific incident in a voice without any emotion and assume they had no emotional response. Recently I told a man who seemed fairly unemotional when he described his accident, 'I'm trying to make sense of this. In all of the reports I have read in your file, you seem to tell your story with no emotion, just like now, while the frank details of what happened to you probably would be terrifying to most people.' His eyes became red and welled up with tears, and then I heard his horror about what happened and how he lives it, vividly, painfully, every day.

I find it is also very important to remain flexible and not fight the other person's chosen direction during an interview. This was made clear to me when I interviewed a young man who came to me carrying a diagnosis of attention deficit hyperactivity disorder. He had also suffered a brain injury and frightened a lot of people because of his impulsivity, sudden rages and tendency towards violence, which had led to several arrests. With me, he was actually quite pleasant and never showed any aggression. However, his thinking was remarkably scattered, as you might expect. Any attempt to use a structured interview would have been futile. His responses to questions typically went in several directions, and he was very energetic and talkative. Questions never really led to answers. So I went along for the ride for several hours, listening carefully and holding the fragments as he told his story in starts and stops and sudden turns, until it gradually emerged amid the apparent confusion.

Some people I work with, like this young man, present with a strong direction, and the flow moves with them like a powerful current. Sometimes it can feel like facing a dam that has burst, but I have never drowned in these rushing waters. I find it best to go with the current and see where it takes me as the other person unfolds his or her story directly and indirectly. I trust they will take me there if I follow patiently and keep my fears and biases in check. It may seem like a lot of information to keep track of when we don't rely on a script or structure but I have worked this way for so long I honestly don't recall a time when I found it onerous. It has flowed naturally from my approach to therapy, which is decidedly non-directive, or what some might describe as classically client-centred. As I experience a person through their unfolding, at their natural pace and in their usual expression, unencumbered by my intruding with structure, a clearer and fuller story reveals itself. The fullness takes shape and holds together.

I rarely use a structured interview, though I find some unique circumstances call for it. In those cases, I am very clear with people about what I am doing when I think it is important to follow a structured format. But generally I don't use a set structure beyond reviewing informed consent, asking questions about the testing that has been done, and then asking questions that help me follow the person's story before, during and after a significant event that may have had an impact on their life and over which there may be a legal action. The most well-known structured interview is the SCID, the Structured Clinical Interview for DSM. The argument for structured interviews is basically that we all miss things when we interview for diagnostic purposes. I think that is probably true. But I think we also all miss things when we use structured interviews.

And so it is an ongoing question. What is it we think is most important not to miss? For me it is most important not to miss the person in front of me. I don't want to ask questions that might get in the way of my seeing the other person more fully or that might focus my further questions in a way that causes me to miss things. We will always miss things, and I think it is important to accept this. Perhaps it is a control issue for each of us to explore, as it relates to ourselves. The question for me is whether I have listened well enough to understand what I need to understand. There is no way I can ask everything and know everything about someone else. It is important not to hold onto that illusion.

Ironically, being concerned about missing things can result in missing things, and sometimes we miss things that are more essential than a diagnostic criterion. I will miss things. You will miss things. We all miss things. Being cross-examined myself as a part of my work has made that abundantly clear to me, and I have had to make peace with that. Part of the pressure we feel may go back to role expectations. If we are doctors, authorities, experts, and our education and training involved being tested on the knowledge we can pull out of our heads, then we are likely to feel a great pressure to know it all and have it all in our heads. We are graded on how much we can pull out of our heads, giving us the message that this is what is valuable about us as clinicians. But we don't have to know it all. We can't possibly know it all, and we don't have to keep it all in our heads. It is OK to consult a reference book in the middle of an assessment, and even in front of a jury when being cross-examined. And if people think less of you because of that, well that is OK too.

So, what do we do with all of this? How do we make further sense of our encounters with other people when our interviews with them are nested within systems? How do we better understand what a person shares with us? I gained some clarity about this process on a recent trip to Kyoto, Japan. While I was there, my husband and I attended a meditation class. I still don't have much of a meditation practice, although I would like to keep returning to it until it is as much a part of my daily life as my much-loved sleep at the end of each day. The class we attended was at Shunko-in, and it was led by Takafumi Kawakami, the Vice Abbot of Myoshinji. Our minds typically are filled with a jumble of thoughts, sometimes repetitive; fragments, eddies and whirlpools made by words streaming on and on. The Vice Abbot spoke to us about meditation as noticing and not judging our thoughts, allowing them to pass, one after another. He pointed out that, while most of us are aware of the way that meditation is used for relaxation, many people only use it for this purpose; they stop right after sitting for meditation and get on with the rest of their day. He explained his view that the real value comes after meditating, when we take the time to reflect on how our bodies feel, as wordlessly as possible, returning our focus to this experience and asking questions like, 'Where do I feel? What is that? Where did it come from, and why?'

Later that night, back at our hotel, it hit me that this is how I approach listening when I do assessment interviews. For me, the key to making full use of an interview is not only listening non-judgementally and following what comes, but also the reflection that takes place afterwards. After observing as non-judgementally as I am able, without getting trapped and getting in the way, fully appreciating what I face, comfortable in my own skin, I allow my experience to continue to wash over me without words, and let questions and words follow from this, rather than lead. As I dictate my notes, I allow myself to be aware of how I am feeling, and this steadily informs me. It can take some time before I start to find words for what happened in the interview. When words and questions lead, we can fool ourselves and lose our full awareness of what is in front of us in the moment. Questions and structures and diagnoses and words become traps that ensnare us and determine our view more narrowly. I find in the end that following brings me greater understanding and insight than leading, structuring and containing. I endeavour to get out of the way during the interview, to follow rather than lead, and reflect on it later.

The quote below is from the United Nation's Istanbul Protocol, in its *Manual on the Effective Investigation and Documentation of Torture and Other Cruel, Inhuman or Degrading Treatment or Punishment*, although I believe it is much more widely applicable:

> (techniques of questioning): Several basic rules must be respected... Information is certainly important, but the person being interviewed is even more so, and listening is more important than asking questions. If you ask only questions, all you get is answers. (1999: 26)

Anything that lessens the humanity of the person we encounter is personal, and the responsibility is ours. In treatment and in assessment interviews, I want to have no goal other than to discover the other person in front of me, to experience them as directly and plainly as possible. This is, of course, much easier said than done, given the multitude of pressures we face simply by working within a system that reinforces so many sources of bias. Beyond our limited senses for taking in the world, we are also faced with powerful distractions that are hidden in plain view and keep us from seeing the people we work with. If we work with people, every aspect of our work is personal. Waking up to this reality is as simple as being willing to ask ourselves questions about the system we work within and being honest with ourselves about what we are doing within it, how it affects us, and how it reinforces our needs.

Questions for me are always the key. What roles are shaping our actions? What goals are being defined because of the system? What are the implications? What is the meaning of time and money for us within the system and how do these drive our actions? How is our method shaped by the system and what processes are shaped by it? If we recognise the manifold influences at play, the interview can be an opportunity to be transparent and real, and to see other people more clearly. As someone I worked with recently said to me, 'It's good when people take the time to listen to what actually goes on.' So simple, yet so difficult.

References

Schutte T (dir) (2016). *Eat That Question: Frank Zappa in his own words.* Sony Pictures Classics.

United Nations (1999). *Manual on the Effective Investigation and Documentation of Torture and Other Cruel, Inhuman or Degrading Treatment or Punishment: Istanbul protocol.* Geneva: United Nations.

9

It's about the power

So how do I make sense of this? How do I explain the fact that I –
with my twenty-five years of experience observing and listening,
being attentive to every clue – was so blind to his condition, so
self-absorbed?
Avishai Lazar (Grossman, 2017)

David Grossman won the Booker International Prize for his novel,
A Horse Walks into a Bar (2017). The central character is a stand-
up comic, but his performance is not what the audience expects. He
offers an unflinching, emotionally raw and honest view of the painful
experiences in life that he still carries. Over the course of the novel,
the audience dwindles as patron after patron heads for the exit. His
friend, a retired judge who has not seen him since they were children,
tries to figure out why he was invited to this performance. Being self-
absorbed, he struggles to get past his own perspective and see his
childhood friend, standing in front of him on the stage, for who he
actually is.

It is easy to blind ourselves to another person's reality by being
self-absorbed. When we go to listen to a comic, we typically want
to be entertained. Meet my expectations, make me laugh, make me
comfortable, and I will pay attention to you. At least, don't bore me
or make me uncomfortable. We come to listen to a comic expecting

comedy, expecting to laugh. We don't expect to encounter a real person with his own struggles, sharing his suffering in a direct and honest way. You're supposed to entertain me and keep me interested, not shock and disturb me. You're not supposed to pull me outside of myself so that I actually see you and your pain. You're not supposed to make me think of realities different from my own. Holding on to our own, insulated reality in this way is about power and our fear of losing it; not just losing it but losing it to another person. And so the other person becomes a threat. Our fear of recognising and sharing reality with other people, acknowledging that our self-absorbed reality does not actually define the world or others, may cause us to head for the exit early.

We are all self-absorbed to some degree, and being self-absorbed blinds us from fully seeing another person. The people we work with might as well be horses that walk into our bar. In other words, another person brings their own reality into our office, into our world and reality. It can be jarring when we fully allow ourselves to recognise this. To deal with the incongruity, we may have to find ways not to see them as horses, not to see them as having entirely different realities from our own. We may fool ourselves that we are observing, listening and being attentive to every clue. It is reflexive and brings comfort to observe from the safety of our reality. It requires other people to conform to us, our theories and diagnoses, rather than require us to make the effort to expand our minds, grow and adapt to the person in front of us. It requires effort and discomfort to accept that our reality will not be theirs. It cannot possibly be theirs. We can have decades of experience and still be blind to the condition of the people who sit right in front of us.

I grew up in a family that tells an ancient story every year in March or April, depending on the moon's cycle. It is a story of blindness to the condition of other people. We celebrate this story with centuries-old rituals, singing songs badly, preparing and eating symbolic and not-so-symbolic foods, and by retelling it together. So, over time, hearing and being a part of this story in this multi-faceted way, it is hard not to see more deeply into it. It is a story that is familiar to many: the Jewish escape from slavery under the Egyptian empire. It is, in part, the story of Moses, who recognises the suffering of the Jewish slaves who are held captive in Egypt. Moses grows up with power and privilege but lets them go to see beyond his own reality. And when he recognises the suffering of other people, he also tries to get the Pharaoh to see past his power and privilege. He tries to impress upon him how he is harming other people. He tells him to do the right thing and release the Jews from slavery.

Unfortunately, despite being faced with a series of plagues, we are told that the Pharaoh's heart remains hardened. He is unable to see beyond his power to recognise the Jewish slaves as people he is harming. It is too late for him. He is too far gone. Power hardens the heart and obscures our capacity to recognise another person's suffering, even when it seems that their suffering should be obvious. Our hardened hearts literally visit plagues upon us while we stubbornly cling to our power and what we know. It brings suffering on us that we ignore. As long as we stay numb, with hardened hearts and wrapped in our comforts, we can never truly be ourselves. Being comfortable in numbness closes off our ability to know ourselves and be comfortable in our own skin. The cost is high: it is a life without knowing or fully being ourselves.

This ancient story is a phenomenal meditation on the nature of privilege, its numbing power and its consequences. Holding a book in our hands allows just enough distance while we let the words into our heads as we are able. I believe that stories such as this hold great power to raise our awareness and help us free our minds. It is a less threatening experience than sitting across from another person who tells us they are suffering, who challenges our comfort while capturing our gaze. Hopefully it is not too late for us.

Possibly the best book I have read on the numbing power of privilege was published in 1908. It is a novel by the great Japanese author Natsume Soseki, entitled *The Miner*. The story is largely an account of the narrator's thoughts as a teenage boy, running away from his wealthy family in Tokyo and eventually finding himself working as a miner with people who are clearly trapped in horrific and dehumanising conditions. He shares his thoughts and observations as he experiences them in what would appear to be profoundly life-changing circumstances. I find it odd that another great Japanese novelist, Haruki Murakami, and the most recent English translator of Soseki's novel, Jay Rubin, have described *The Miner* as a novel about nothing. I continue to be stirred by its radical message. It is hardly a novel about nothing. It is a profound exploration of human nature and the numbing power of privilege, with its inevitable gravitational pull that hardens the human heart. This message is made all the more clear when we realise the narrator is an older man, once again ensconced in the comforts of his wealth and privilege and reflecting back on this time in his youth. His ugly, dehumanising judgements of those living in poverty appear to be utterly unchanged, despite having come face to face with the suffering of other people living in poverty and actually living through that suffering himself. The theme of privilege as an unchangeable force in the lives of those who are trapped within it seems to me to be captured perfectly at the outset of the novel, when the young runaway remarks, 'No point walking if the trees aren't going to do something – develop. Better to stay put and try to outstare a tree, see who laughs first' (Soseki, 2015: 27).

Privilege bestows numbness; numbness protects privilege. One of the consequences of our numbness is that: 'If you are numb, you will not be able to gauge whether or not you're doing harm'. I heard Laura van Dernoot Lipsky (2015) say this in a repeat broadcast of her TEDx Talk on CBC radio during my morning commute. She was discussing the impact on us when we work with traumatised people, the impact on us when we face suffering in other people. I had to pull over and write down her words. Our numbness makes the harm we inflict easy to ignore. Awareness is the key to addressing our numbness and not harming other people and ourselves with it, but the numbness itself makes it so hard to see. It is a circular trap. Our privilege, our unearned comfort, gets in the way of seeing our hearts as hardened. Our need to see ourselves as good people only adds to the difficulty. We like to think that only an evil person has a hardened heart; only an evil person is numb to the suffering of other people around them. It is easy not to recognise this in ourselves, which is the problem with numbness. Given the very real and present suffering all around us, suffering that seems impossible to do something about, given what we may see as our own smallness and limited lifespan, going numb also seems like a reasonably self-protective act. Yet when we do not recognise that we are numb, we enter our therapy or assessment work incapable of being fully present to the person we are facing, unable to gauge the harm we may be doing.

If you are reading my words, you too are trapped within some form of privilege: racial, economic, gender, age, sexual orientation, physical ability etc. I am also trapped, so I am not writing this as a judgement. It is my observation of our human condition. It is simply what I see when I look at myself and people around me. I do not hold any illusion that I have somehow escaped. This does not make you a bad person, though the impulse may be to deny the power we carry with us into our life situations, including our work with other people. We may be loath to admit it, but we all have hardened hearts to some extent. The real work, the hard work, ever present, is learning about it and trying to soften what we can soften whenever we can. When we let go of power, our treasured comfort we have been hoarding, our hearts can soften and new worlds open up to us.

The necessary journey from self-absorbed to self-aware is not a journey from A to B. It would not fit neatly into a Newtonian equation. It is a journey of continual return, refocusing and recommitting to awareness, shifting patterns of awareness and returning numbness. The challenge is finding a way to be more self-aware, to commit to returning on a regular basis in this very personal search. It may be useful to find guiding principles along the way in this meandering journey that knows no end and circles back on itself. One place to find them can be in the words of a prophet like Moses. If it is easier, just think of Moses as a sage, or at least wise. It may also be easy to think of his story as a myth, a guiding story that you are under no pressure to take literally, which is how I see it.

After one of his encounters with the interconnectedness and oneness of things, Moses shared 10 utterances that still pervade the thinking of many. I have come to see them more as counsel or good advice than commandments. Among these utterances, he guided us to honour our mother and father. There are many understandings of this. For me, it is a foundational attitude in coming to know myself. What better place to begin than trying to understand my parents? As I get older, the perspective that comes with age brings increasing clarity. It is easier to look beyond the powerful role of parent and see the actual people who brought me into the world and raised me. This is especially so as I look back on my memories of them and reflect on memories of myself at the same ages they once were. The meaning of my memories shifts, as does my awareness of who my parents are and my understanding of myself. I increasingly see myself reflected in my parents. I recognise myself and I learn about myself by paying attention to them and my memories of them. Even in my ideas that led to this book I can see the sudden jumps in thinking that I notice in my mom, and the tendency to get lost in the wonder of a single word, like my dad. When I have conflict or when I get annoyed with them, if I am honest, I can usually find some reflection of those traits or behaviours in myself, and my heart softens. Of course, it is easier to be annoyed with someone else, easier to be self-absorbed and not face my annoyance with myself. It is more comfortable that way. And we all may remain there, comfortably numb.

Honouring my mother and father, to me, also means honouring my heritage, knowing where I came from and how this shapes my view of the world. My name carries part of this journey. During my master's studies, a professor asked us to write down three words that described us. No one wrote their name – an interesting lesson. We may carry our names throughout our lives without reflecting on their importance with respect to our identities. Most of my friends know me as Brian, some call me Bri, and my sister still calls me Bri Bri. For a Jew who was born in the Midwest in the United States, Brian is a name of assimilation, and this awareness can be a rich avenue for exploration.

I also have a Hebrew name, and it means a lot to me: Baruch Yaakov. The name literally means Blessed Jacob. Jacob is described in ancient stories as a flawed man who deceived his father to get a blessing that should have been given to his brother. Blessed Jacob. However, he is also described as a man who wrestled with an angel, a metaphorical struggle with God, an existential struggle. For this, he also was blessed and given the name Israel: he who struggles with God. This was a blessing he earned, a blessing he worked for. Blessed Jacob. As a child, I always liked the sound of the name Baruch Yaakov, but it has come to mean more and more to me as I wander through life and struggle with what I see, while enjoying and appreciating what I have, knowing that much of it I never directly earned: blessings earned and unearned. My name is a very personal reminder to me of the place privilege has in my life, as well as my ties to my ancestors.

We might ask ourselves how we name ourselves and what power our names have to shape us. The power of recognising our names goes beyond our actual names to the things we call ourselves. I call myself a Jew. I call myself gay, or queer, depending on who I am with. I call myself doctor, psychologist and clinician. I call myself American, and also Canadian. I call myself non-directive, client-centred and person-centred. I also call myself white and a man, with all that comes with unpacking these names and understanding the power and privilege they bring me – power and privilege I have received through no special effort of my own.

I define and redefine myself, and I recognise that I am more than the names I give myself. I am also, certainly, more than the names other people give me and use to see me. We are all unique intersections of all that has come before us and all that we have seen. We owe a debt that cannot be repaid to all who came before us and those who surround us. The words we use are not ours and we come into languages that are waiting for us to learn them. I have not invented a single word. When we start to recognise this more fully, we may be more open to the ways our parents, our ancestors and our culture live on through us. The way I think and feel is not exactly mine. I could assert ownership of it but I know that something much larger finds its expression in my small life.

For much of my life, I have read Jewish writers and spiritual texts and Jewish authors of fiction who understand the nuances of Jewish identity. Time and again I find myself in the words expressed by other people. I rediscover myself. I feel and think like a Jew. Of course, I also feel and think like an American. There are many aspects of my identity that are sources of nourishment. And I find, time and again, whatever leads me back to myself makes me more comfortable encountering other people and allows me greater comfort with what leads them back to themselves. Only when we are better at seeing ourselves will we become better at seeing others. To honour other people, to honour their parents and their heritage, I must always return to my own. If I am not able to do this, how can I ever hope to see other people and how their worlds are shaped by where they come from? How odd to think that someone sitting across from me could possibly share the same reality and experience as my own. How self-absorbed. How absurd.

When we start to move beyond self-absorbed to self-aware, we move beyond the need to see ourselves and to be seen as a good person, beyond holding tightly to privilege and our perspective. While there is, of course, privilege with respect to race, age, gender, sexual orientation and on and on, there is also privilege in seeing all of our work with other people, including who they are, through our own reality and world view – through our own belief systems, our own theories, our own diagnostic frameworks, our own roles and goals. We are self-absorbed when we do this. We may have good intentions but when we don't understand how we impose them, they come from being self-absorbed. And that is how we begin to pave that fabled road. Identity and privilege: we bring these into the room, and the relationship, whether or not we are aware of it or acknowledge it. When we don't acknowledge it, the problem is being self-absorbed. Usually we don't acknowledge it because we think it reflects badly on us, that it reflects everything about us, and we don't want to be a bad person.

Rather than being self-absorbed, we must learn to be more self-aware, so that we can become other-absorbed. Otherwise we risk seeing people as an expression of our understanding of the world, making them an extension of ourselves. The further risk in this is that, when we are afraid and feel our power is threatened, we may tend to make people an extension of what we fear in ourselves and then do something to contain and control them. Do we engage in a struggle to recognise our self-absorption or remain self-absorbed at the expense of other people and ourselves?

I lived through several decades oblivious to my numbness, to the hardening of my heart. That began to change when I met Dr Samellah Abdullah. I was lucky enough to study in a doctoral psychology programme that had a significant experiential component, including a year-long extended group process experience that culminated in a marathon group weekend. At that final weekend of the course, I had a difficult experience with overt homophobia that was angrily expressed towards me. I felt decidedly vulnerable and unsafe. Because of that experience, I was looking for community, a place to heal, or at least to retreat safely.

Dr Abdullah had created a safe space for the students of colour, who experienced expressions of racism throughout the year, to gather that weekend. There was nothing similar for queer students, and I wandered in, not thinking about being white. I was self-absorbed. The people in the group were very kind to me, but my presence, simply being white, was impacting on them. Dr Abdullah looked at me and I still remember the warmth in her face. She gently said, 'Do you see what is happening in here?' Although the students gathered there welcomed me, I recognised what was happening. That experience remains with me 25 years later. That one question was transformative. I knew I had much to learn, and I still do.

The next year, I took Dr Abdullah's class, an experiential process group addressing treatment issues with diverse populations. I will be forever grateful to her for the lessons she taught me. Among the most important, she gave me a process to explore my stereotypes and their impact on me and on those I encounter. She gave me a way of seeing myself and the world that I cannot unsee. She gave me a recognition of the folly of which I am often guilty, as are many, of seeing ourselves as the heroes of our own life stories, which then casts others in less desirable roles. How much more honest to recognise that I can be a schmuck and I have flaws, and to be alright with that reality as I strive to do better, than to deny it and retreat to a place of comfort where everyone else is bad. I still see the value of leaning into the discomfort. That really is where the growth is.

Stereotypes are powerful things. Our stereotypes are triggered when our power is threatened. They are meant to help us survive. We appear to be 'wired' that way. But there is no actual threat when we face someone in our work who is different from us. We make it real, without thinking about it. This can be subtle when we have stereotypes of others who are different from us in some way. This is especially true if we have not taken the time to turn our focus back on ourselves and explore the stereotypes we hold that may get activated in an encounter with another person. A knee-jerk defensiveness is usually the main reason we don't take a look at this within ourselves. We don't want to see ourselves as bad.

Holding stereotypes is not bad, though this is what many of us fear and what drives us to deny we hold them. We may even get angry at someone for suggesting we do. Also, if we spend most of our time with people who seem more like us, we may live with the bias of a worldview that goes unchallenged. We carry this with us when we meet others who are different from us, assuming they see the world as we do. There is great potential for being able to see other people more clearly when we learn to examine our stereotypes and how they are triggered and how they get in the way of seeing other people. This is, to my mind, a much more fruitful approach to understanding diversity and being open to realities different from our own. It requires a lot more of us than the museum or catalogue approach, which basically entails studying a laundry list of what are supposed to be values, traits, beliefs, behaviours etc in various cultures. That approach ends up being another way of controlling through categorising, objectifying other people to place them in the internal museums in our brains. It keeps us from real encounter. Becoming self-aware, aware of our inner demons and how it may be easier for us to see others as these very demons, can help us gain comfort in being other-absorbed, to give up our power over other people.

Like a novel, a photograph should be less of a threat than being with another person face to face. We can put it down or look away. Even so, it still may be hard to see what is there if we can't get past being self-absorbed, past the need to see or experience everything on our terms, the comfort of our numbness. I recently revisited a photograph of Dr Martin Luther King, Jr (O'Neill, 2010), wearing a suit, tie and hat, looking straight into the camera, his arm held forcibly behind his back by a white police officer. His wife is standing nearby, watching. He was arrested simply for trying to attend the trial of another civil rights leader. It is a clear image of racism, institutionalised and otherwise. As he looks through the camera, it is as if he reaches through time, so powerful is his gaze; as if it is happening right now. And, of course, it is. And, of course, it is not.

The look on his face is filled with meaning, and I often find myself transfixed by it. There is something transcendent about his gaze, and a power that is almost palpable in that transcendence. Meeting his eyes, I meet many things in myself – who I have been, who I am now, and where I am heading. How would I have understood his eyes and that scene when I was younger? This man's gaze impresses an important reality on anyone willing to gaze back. Or we can miss it entirely. The more I return his gaze, the more I begin to take in the reality around him and what his experience might be, the power over him that is being exercised, the easy stance of power around him, the lack of recognition of his humanity, his awareness that this is unfolding. His eyes hold so much and look right at us. I wonder if he might be thinking, 'Do you see what is happening? Do you really see what is happening?' Of course, I will never know and could never guess this great man's thoughts. And that doesn't matter when I face him in this photograph that reaches across a half century. What matters, it seems to me, is that I do not let my issues get in the way of seeing his humanity and what is happening in that moment; that I allow myself to step back in order to bring him into focus.

It is one of the most extraordinary photographs I have come across. And yet it is just a photograph. It is easy to approach it at my own pace and to keep a safe distance. It is easy to stop looking. No one will know. However, with the people we encounter in our work, we are not only looking, observing and wondering; we also are listening and interacting in a relationship. We can be present to the experience other people are having in the moment and check with them to see if we understood them. They are not photographs that cannot respond. It is a simple act, but perhaps not a common one, to check our understanding of someone with them, from a place within ourselves of yielding to their authority over their own experience. It is simple to ask, 'Did I understand you correctly?'

References

Grossman D (2017). *A Horse Walks into a Bar* (Cohen J, trans). New York, NY: Vintage International.

O'Neill C (2010). Charles Moore, photographer of the Civil Rights Movement, dies at 79. [Online.] *NPR*; 16 March. www.npr.org/sections/pictureshow/2010/03/charles_moore.html?t=1558610910424 (accessed 17 November 2018).

Soseki N (2015). *The Miner* (Rubin J, trans). London: Aardvark Bureau.

van Dernoot Lipsky L (2015). *Beyond the Cliff.* [Video.] YouTube. www.youtube.com/watch?v=uOzDGrcvmus (accessed 17 November 2018).

10
Fear itself

I must not fear.
Fear is the mind-killer.
Fear is the little-death that brings total obliteration.
I will face my fear.
I will permit it to pass over me and through me.
And when it has gone past I will turn the inner eye to see its path.
Where the fear has gone there will be nothing.
Only I will remain.
Bene Gesserit litany against fear (Herbert, 2010)

Franklin Delano Roosevelt was on to something. Although, realistically, I think most of us are not comforted by the thought that the only thing we have to fear is fear itself. Fear is an intense emotional state and there is much that is frightening in this world. We each are uniquely and exquisitely vulnerable to certain fears. If we lived in constant fear, always aware of what frightens us most, we likely would stop functioning. So we are in some sense blessed with ways of ignoring those fears. But our fears are there, often just out of sight, and likely influencing us far more than we may realise. Their influence is even greater when we do not recognise them.

Our work with other people presents us with endless possibilities for encounters with our fears. I have been increasingly aware of this since entering the field, but the turning point for me was when I was asked to do assessments for men who were renditioned, imprisoned and tortured. When I got through the process and found ways to make sense of it, and then found ways to heal myself, I also found I was a different clinician. I found myself more comfortable in my vulnerability and in my ability to face horrific pain in other people and what it brings up in me. Up to that point, I had faced what some people might consider frightening in the various people I had worked with. And I also faced what many might consider ordinary, but it was frightening to me when I was just beginning to do the hard work of encountering other people. One of my earliest experiences in the field was working with students who were dealing with everyday stressors. The work was frightening for me because of my lack of experience and confidence, because of my lack of comfort in my own skin. I doubt I encountered people deeply when I first began this work. Every day gets a little bit closer.

At different stages of my career, I have been asked, 'How can you do that kind of work?' How can you work with people diagnosed with schizophrenia? How can you work with psychotic people? How can you work with people with developmental disabilities? How can you work with old people with dementia? How can you work with people who are grieving a loved one who was killed? How can you work with people who have lost limbs? How can you work with people who are disfigured? How can you work with people who were tortured? How can you work with people living with chronic pain? How can you work with… *them*? These are good questions, and questions I think we all should face honestly as clinicians, because it is necessary to face our fears in order to be empathically engaged with people in our work. If we are not able to be open to what it might be like to be in painful and frightening situations, we are not going to really see the people who come into our offices. But that means getting close to those experiences as if they could be ours.

I have sat and faced pain in other people for about a quarter of a century now. I have listened to people tell me about torture, rape, facing death, being in constant and excruciating pain, being disfigured, seeing suicide as their only option. I have consistently found that real life is more frightening than the most convincing movie or book, especially when real life comes into my office and faces me. The experiences people share with me are truly horrific. A man's hand is stuck in a conveyor belt, crushing it. He reaches in with his other hand to pull it out, and both hands are then mangled and stuck. He screams for help for 20 minutes until someone hears him, and it is another 20 minutes before an emergency crew can remove him. He is left with hands that are disfigured and do not function, and chronic pain that always reminds him of the stunning horror of what happened to him.

A man is renditioned to a Middle Eastern prison, where he is brutally tortured, physically and psychologically, for two years, and can recount what was done to him as clearly as if it had just happened. Parents find out their daughter was sucked out of the passenger window of a truck and shredded by another truck across 100 metres of highway. A father watches helplessly as his son is pulled by rushing flood waters into a drainage pipe and drowned. A man is thrown from his car, suffers severe injuries and watches, unable to do anything, as his girlfriend, trapped inside, burns to death. A driver is hit head-on by a truck and sees his friend thrown from the passenger seat. He finds him dead on the roadside and now struggles on a daily basis with the impact of brain injury, chronic pain and intrusive images of his dead friend.

I am not writing this simply to be provocative. And I am not embellishing. These are the real things that happen to real people, who then come into my office and see me, and I must be able to see them. I must be able to face them fully. What we do with our fears when we face other people determines how fully we will see other people for who they are and what they are experiencing.

Fear does not have to be of the heart-pounding, oh-my-God-I'm-going-to-die variety. In fact, I think in our work that type of fear experience is likely to be fairly rare for most of us. Fear is much more likely to present itself as the subtle wariness or discomfort that signals us to take action before it gets anywhere near heart-pounding, oh my God, I'm going to die. Many of us have learned about the fight or flight reaction that is wired into us and other animals. We tend to think of this occurring only in terrifying, life-or-death circumstances. But the way we fight or flee when we pick up on traces of threat is likely to appear somewhat ordinary and may pass unnoticed, at least by us. I think many people we work with recognise what we are doing when we turn on them or tune them out, even when we don't realise we are doing this.

The most common flight action we may take is to go numb. Perhaps we numb ourselves by getting into our heads and intellectualising. Perhaps we just don't see what is right in front of us or disconnect from what we feel immediately within ourselves. Or we may fight. Again, we may be so close to our behaviours that we do not recognise we are fighting. We may fight by trying to change other people according to what we think is good. We may fight by categorising or diagnosing people. These objectifying acts are subtle acts of violence that we may all too easily slip into. We may also be resistant to recognising them as aggressive. Not hearing what a person says and going numb does harm indirectly. It is not quite as bad as covering our ears and shouting, 'I can't hear you! I can't hear you!' But it is not much better. Whether we fight or flee, we are doing harm to the people we work with.

When we face another person in our work, we face the unknown. We face uncertainty. We may struggle with a subtle fear that we will lose control of the situation and, worse yet, the person sitting in front of us will gain control, will be the one with power. Anything could happen. We may feel compelled to shrink the number of possibilities, since the idea of anything happening can be frightening. So we may force a structure on the encounter – a structured clinical interview, a manualised form of treatment, a technique or a diagnostic mindset. We determine the ground rules, how things should unfold and proceed, what is acceptable. When we first start out doing this kind of work, facing other people, we may struggle because of how inexperienced we are, so we may turn to other structures that were made by people with more experience, such as interview and therapy techniques. Interestingly, when we become more experienced, we may find ourselves trying to cultivate or return to a beginner's mind, but from a place that is more grounded because of facing people over and over again. While experience may bring a sense of comfort in our own skin, it can also bring years of built-up defences of which we are unaware that keep us distant in different ways than when we first began this work.

The more we pride ourselves on our knowledge and expertise, backed up by degrees and titles and certificates, the more vulnerable we may be to our fear of not knowing, our fear of facing the unknown. We can become very afraid of looking stupid. The cost seems greater. The fall seems higher. Graduate training doesn't help matters, as we are supervised and graded on our mastery of concepts, on our knowing, on looking competent and intelligent. Being stupid typically is not embraced as a good starting point in our daily work with other people. We are supposed to be smart. Our fear of not knowing things, of looking stupid, of seeing ourselves as stupid, creates barriers between us and what is real in the moment.

Being stupid actually may be the best place to start, or the best stance to return to on a regular basis. Being aware of what we don't know and acknowledging it is freeing and powerful. If I don't have to be afraid of being stupid, then maybe I can listen more attentively when you talk about things I don't know. Maybe I can let you teach me. If I don't feel I have to come up with brilliant or good answers when I am asked a question, I can hear it more fully. And sometimes saying that I don't know is the best and most honest answer I can give.

There is an odd flip side, a type of flight we might take with some people we work with when we face them and don't know what to do. These people may become our 'difficult patients'. They are somehow unco-operative or unable to engage in treatment. However, when we don't feel the need to fight or run away, there are no 'difficult patients'. One of the radical things about Garry Prouty's Pre-Therapy is the way it challenges the notion that some people can't be reached. I believe this is the more important message of his work, rather than a focus on how to do it in a manualised way.

We also hear about people who come into our offices who are not psychologically minded. I attended a conference during which a psychiatrist talked about patients not being psychologically minded. He said, 'We can't do much for them.' I believe the real problem lies not in the people we face in our work but in psychologists and psychiatrists not being psychologically minded and facing our fears. When we see a lack of change or progress or movement as the other person's fault, we save our sense of dignity. Our expertise remains unchallenged and we don't have to look stupid. It's good to be king.

Pain is one of the many things that can make us feel powerless, incompetent, incapable and useless. It is also the most common complaint people bring to their doctors. My work these days is literally with pain. Most of the people I face in my office are living with chronic and severe pain. Usually they also are struggling with being depressed, anxious and traumatised. Their pain is all-encompassing. Unfortunately, even pain has been concretised and categorised in healthcare and in daily life, making it something we have, something we are in, or something that is in us. We make pain into something we can point to and see over there. Psychology has been moving beyond the simplistic and outdated view of pain as something that is purely physical for many decades now, particularly since the ground-breaking work of Melzack and Wall (1965) that pointed towards an understanding of pain being biopsychosocial. Biopsychosocial. That is a mouthful of a word, but in many ways it expresses a view of pain that is not constricted or confined to something we see as purely physical, like tissue damage, or something we see as purely emotional, like grief.

Pain is physical. Pain is psychological. Pain is social. Pain is multi-faceted. Pain is subjective. Yet we still often think of it in more Cartesian ways, splitting the mind and body even though we know that our experience of pain comes from the brain, which is fully integrated in our body and aware of and functioning within our social context. Our diagnostic manuals have attempted to move away from the Cartesian, dualist view, and generally have done a poor job of it. Our understanding of a mind-body split with respect to how we see and understand pain is a habit that keeps us from the fullness of pain. It keeps us a step removed and makes pain a little less frightening. The challenge is to find a way to talk about pain without needing to distance ourselves, smooth it over, or to look for something redemptive or positive. It is a natural inclination to offer something concrete or positive in the face of something frightening or painful or hard to hear, but it also shuts down the other person's expression. It is a way of negating it and not giving it space to be heard and fully appreciated. The person we are working with is not in that much pain. They are experiencing less pain objectively than they express subjectively. They are over-reporting, exaggerating or lying. These can often be fictions we tell ourselves to feel good, adding to the suffering of the people we work with.

There is an immediacy to real pain, an intensity that adds to our perception of threat. It carries a force that can make us recoil. We may sense that, if we face it, we too will feel it. We may fear we will feel it too intensely. Abraham Joshua Heschel, the great theologian and civil rights activist, spoke of the beauty of the scars on his heart that he carried by opening himself to the suffering of other people (Heschel, 2007). This has always resonated with me. I find myself asking how I can open my heart to intense pain and not be consumed by it, so that I can hear it and come back and tell the story as fully and accurately as possible. Without opening my heart to the other person's experience of pain and suffering, can I ever really see and understand them? Can I bear a wound to my heart and stay connected, not get lost in the moment, and not get lost over time to burnout, awash in pain and suffering? I often hear myself saying that the day I can no longer allow my heart to be scarred is the day I will have to leave this field. I hope that day never comes.

At the same time, I must be able to step back and ask what just happened. I have to find a distance to reflect in relative calm on what I just experienced. People come to us and share their stories. And stories always carry some type of truth. It's just that we are not always so literate. Some of us may be shockingly illiterate. Sometimes we are either too scared or too sloppy or too self-absorbed to read carefully, and the story's meaning escapes us. If we hope to encounter other people fully, we have to be willing to face that our hearts will be scarred. We have to trust that we can carry those metaphorical scars and still see clearly enough and be strong enough to understand and bear the burden of another person's story, another person's pain.

The need to cover over pain and walk away from it seems to me so very human, and very common. It is more comfortable to look for the good, the happy, the noble, the uplifting, the positive. I think ultimately fear is behind this – fear of imagining horrible things, painful things, happening to ourselves. Push it away. Grey skies are gonna clear up, put on a happy face. It may be obvious, but I am not a fan of happy endings in movies and books. That's why I don't usually watch films that come out of Hollywood, that lead us towards the uplifting message, smoothing over a reality that is not always comfortable and can leave us disturbed and frightened. I don't see pain and suffering as an opportunity to push other people to focus on hope. I think it is important to face the pain with eyes wide open, not immediately look for something uplifting to ease it, look for the good in the person's situation, or look for them to be a hero for living with it. Feel-good movies are a wonderful escape and heroes can inspire us and remind us of what is best in us, that we can always strive to do better. The problem is when we see the need for happy endings in all aspects of our life or we look too often for an escape, and then bring this into our work with other people. When we feel the need to make someone stronger or braver in the moment, perhaps because we are afraid and need them to be strong and brave, we rob them of the importance of their experience in the moment. This is true even when that experience is one of vulnerability, fear and pain. Sitting with another person in the depth of their pain and suffering may be frightening and uncomfortable, but it has very real value. We have to ask ourselves why we might need to change that or escape from it so quickly or so often, before really seeing what is there and being with the other person fully in those moments.

Of course, there is nothing wrong with looking for the good or recognising a person's strength, but if it comes from us first, I wonder about what we have done to make ourselves comfortable rather than actually help the person with pain who is facing us. It seems dangerous to me, and also disrespectful, to move too quickly past suffering and horror in order to experience comfort. It may seem counter-intuitive at first, but the horror of encountering one life fully can be heavier than considering pain on a mass scale. Thinking of pain on a mass scale adds an inherent element of the unthinkable and moves us away from the intensity of an individual life. It creates distance and lessens the impact. The single life is easier to grasp. It is easier to imagine that life as our own. As a result, it is more frightening and easier to run away from. It may be more painful to face the immediate suffering of one person in a face-to-face encounter if we open our hearts to the fullness of it. We may think we are doing a good thing by changing someone's story with our techniques, our structured or manualised listening or our own sense of what is good or correct or the best thing to do. By doing this, we ultimately make people into products of our own reality. When I think of it this way, it doesn't sound like a good thing to do.

In one of the first groups I led as a young psychologist, a personal growth group, a white woman was having great difficulty acknowledging that a black woman was different from her. I found myself imagining her only encountering herself in other people; a somewhat surreal image. But I took her comments to the logical extreme in this image and asked her what it would be like if everyone in the group were actually exactly the same as her. She looked somewhat stunned at first, and then said she thought that would be a psychotic experience. Something shifted for her and she began seeing the other woman more clearly as different from herself. Seeing difference is a threat to our sense of value and integrity, perhaps our very existence as unique beings. It may be hard to acknowledge that another unique being could have just as much value, that their very different reality could be as correct and fully lived in as our own. We intellectually get it that we are all unique, but experiencing it is a different thing and can be very threatening. This leads us to the very scary fear of facing ourselves.

I recognise something of my own experiences in the more extreme distress people bring in when they see me in my office. The thought of some of the difficult things I experience from day to day being more severe or ever-present is threatening. What if the anxiety I feel in the moment didn't end? What if it grew louder, crowding out other feelings and thoughts? What if this momentary struggle with getting motivated, unable to find the initiative to do anything, hesitant to get out of bed, feeling no drive or interest, lasted all day, all week, all year, with no end in sight, only getting worse? What if the pain I feel when my back goes out never goes away? What if this one day I am spending on the floor on a heating pad, wincing with every little movement of my body, unable to do anything, stretched on for years? Attempting to be empathic draws on my own experiences and the powers of my imagination to expand or worsen that experience, to extrapolate and face a potentially frightening future that presses in on me in the present moment. It forces me to face my own vulnerability. It is a threat to the integrity of my being, the possibility of being undone, losing control or in some way being utterly destroyed.

What we generally might fear in ourselves are those things we judge as bad, dirty, evil, frightening and horrible. Those are hard things to face and acknowledge carrying around. They are hard to accept as integral to our being. Freud's brilliance in part was to shine a light on who we are as human beings and our need to avoid facing our fullness. It is much easier, much more comfortable, to see ourselves as good. It is threatening and can be painful to recognise the bad things in us. Facing it requires a loving attitude towards ourselves, an acceptance and a moving beyond judgement that is quite difficult to achieve and is likely to be an ongoing and sometimes messy process. But if I can't face something in myself, if I find it too frightening, I will never be able to face it and begin to see and understand it in someone else. Fear is the mind killer.

We all have our comforts in this field – places and people we gravitate towards. We also tend to be aware of obvious discomforts, and not so aware of those that are less obvious. Facing the unknown is a source of discomfort. Almost 20 years ago, I began working with people living with chronic pain complicated by other layers and sources of distress. I was not immediately comfortable facing people with chronic pain, disfigurement and traumatic grief. For five years or so, it was wearing on me and draining me, and I wondered if I was actually suited for this work. I had to take time out for myself to understand what was happening, and I had to find other people who could help me make sense of it. And something shifted, so that I now find I can be with people much more fully and not be drained and undone by the experience. My work now feels simply like an acknowledgment that what I see, what I hear and what I face in the people sitting across from me is reality. This is life. And my work allows me to be very present to life on a regular basis. I am grateful to be able to see it this way, to experience this sort of acceptance. I am also very aware that I have limitations; there is only so much I can absorb. It is good to know when you have had your fill, so to speak. Even better is knowing before you have had your fill and learning how to step back and take care of yourself. At the end of the day, sitting silently with my husband or having wordless conversations with my dog is just about right. But when I encounter people in my work, I do my best to get beyond my fears and my need for comfort so I can hear fully what is real that another person is trying to share with me. I have been rewarded richly by this very human experience. My life is fuller, and more fully lived, because of it.

Facing pain and facing our fears begins with facing the present moment and showing up. Distractions are everywhere, and we carry many within us at all times. Our work always comes back to knowing ourselves and finding an acceptance or comfort in our own skin so we can be with other people. We may be tired or sleepy, hungry, thirsty, carrying our own pains or living with our own illnesses. Our minds can be a swirl of emotions and thoughts that are always there, even when the volume is not so loud, and we are easily snared by them. We may be aware of time, our next appointment or what awaits us when our work is over. We may find ourselves frustrated, angry or bored, and, as distractions go, these are certainly red flags that deserve honest reflection. Our distractions are subtle temptations that become easy places to hide and then get lost.

Thinking about how distractions can interfere with our ability to encounter others, my memories take me back to my post-doctoral training, when I consulted with Barbara Brodley. I brought a very specific and concrete question to her about being distracted while doing therapy. The question was also of a somewhat personal nature, and I can still hear Barbara's uniquely warm voice: 'Brian, if you need to pee, you should go and pee.' I wonder now what she would think about my including that in this book. Two years of supervision with one of the leading experts in the client-centred approach, and this is what I include about my time with her. I'd like to think she would smile. I think her response is actually a very profound statement about recognising and dealing with our distractions so that we can be present. I think that is why her words stay with me all these years later. Doctors become doctors, psychologists become psychologists, clinicians become clinicians, and therapists become therapists when we face our distractions and we face ourselves. So be afraid. Be very afraid. And face your fears.

References

Herbert F (2010). *Dune*. New York, NY: Ace.

Heschel AJ (2007). *Moral Grandeur and Spiritual Audacity: reflections on the life and thought of Abraham Joshua Heschel*. [The Lillian and Marvin Goldblatt Jewish Studies Lectures]. Hamilton, ON: McMaster University.

Melzack R, Wall PD (1965). Pain mechanisms: a new theory. *Science 150*(3699): 971–979.

Conclusion
Egoless practice

Embrace your inner idiot
Garry Prouty (personal communication)

Listening is harder than speaking. Speaking comes from something inside of us that we direct towards other people and is often a process we don't really think about when we are engaged in it. It can also come from a patient and deliberate focus on our thoughts, which we may hear as an inner voice, allowing us to deliver measured and well-crafted sentences. We may hear this voice before we let it out, or we may be unaware of hearing it, speaking freely and perhaps mindlessly.

When I write, I am much more aware of this inner process as I sit in silence and listen to my thoughts. Over time, I have become better acquainted with it. Sometimes it is a jumble, buckshot, a kaleidoscope – thoughts, images, feelings, memories, songs, associations, all caught up in the flow and vying for my attention. And sometimes there is just one clear line that runs smoothly and simply. I listen and let it out onto the page, trusting I can edit later, engaging in a discussion between my inner voice and my voice on the page. My hope is that I will be able to find enough clarity so that my words will unfold in your mind in a meaningful way. I experience the source when I speak as the same as the source when I write. It is lifelong flow of internal ramblings and babblings and commentary. It is far easier to focus on or give ourselves over to this inner voice, to identify with it, believe in it and agree with it. Agreeing with ourselves is easy and brings comfort. We often don't recognise we are doing this. Our beliefs, our influences, our fears and our emotions, our experiences and our unexamined identity all find expression, regardless of how aware we are of this happening. Speaking generally comes from this self-absorbed place.

Listening also comes from something inside of us but has the added dimension of a focus on something outside of us. We tend to think about listening as being only about what comes from outside of us, but the quality of our listening is determined by what comes from inside of us. It is determined by what we do with our filters, our internal distractors, our tendency to be self-absorbed. It rests on our identification with belief systems and theories. It depends on how concretely or firmly we hold on to the meanings that words have for us. It depends on our capacity to appreciate difference, our capacity to value a reality that is as precious as our own. It also depends on how we face our fears. When we listen to another person, they offer an external source of information, but we may remain focused on our inner voice and filters rather than being focused on the unique reality being expressed by someone distinctly outside of us. We look for what is within us to grasp what is coming from the other person. We tend towards what is internal because we must. We can't experience the other person's experience. Unfortunately, we also tend to be self-absorbed, having spent most of our lives with the constant presence, the constant chatter, of what is within us. What is within us is exquisitely familiar and comfortable. We define what we hear from other people in our own words, imbued with our own meanings, and create the conditions for hearing it, rather than letting go enough to let other people define themselves.

If I see myself in my work with other people as a listener, an observer, a witness to another person's experience, as someone attempting as accurately as possible to understand the person I am encountering, I must learn to take on a stance of disinterest in myself. Being disinterested in myself does not mean being unaware of myself and my experiences, as these will remain an integral part of my listening. Rather, it means being disinterested in personal gain, in looking like a professional, in looking like a scientist, in looking like an expert, in saving the other person, or in catching the other person in a lie. It means being willing to let go of my need for power and comfort. It means not running towards numbness. I have to be comfortable enough in my own skin not to flee or fight.

For the relatively brief time I am with another person, I want as much as possible to understand them beyond a role I might take on. Being disinterested in myself, I can become more fully interested in the person I am encountering. My goal, as much as possible, if I am trying to understand other people, is to let go of my attachments, my tendency to be self-absorbed, so that I can be more other-absorbed. In this sense, my goal is to become egoless in my work with other people. Some days I come closer to meeting this goal than on others. It is a goal that is always just out of reach that I hope as much as possible to strive towards. I don't expect ever to achieve this state of being but I find it reasonable to expect myself to move increasingly in the direction of being egoless when I listen to other people in my work. I think it is also reasonable to expect that I will fall short, and reasonable to want to keep trying to do better.

Why strive to be egoless in our work with other people? Quite simply, it is the decent thing to do. For me the question more worthy of exploration is how to move in the direction of being egoless in my work. Humility may be the best starting point. Humility means knowing and embracing our limits and recognising the limits of what we cling to. Knowing the limits of our professional competence is one of the central values found in the ethical codes that guide our field. I believe we should consider extending this ethical principle to being aware of our limitations more broadly as human beings and the limitations of the things we cling to when we face another person in our work. Let go of the need to appear intelligent, the need to be the expert, the need to analyse, the need to be in control. Don't take ourselves too seriously. Don't take our beliefs, our science and our theories too seriously.

I know I'm an idiot and I know I often fall short, and this awareness keeps me grounded. Perhaps that is where I should have started this book. Perhaps that is the only necessary lesson. I don't say this just to be self-deprecating or self-effacing. Nor do I believe it is the only truth about me. But it is an important truth to tell. I believe it is never too late to acknowledge this important reality and plainly state it. We may not be aware of how routinely we see ourselves as the hero of our own story, and it can be a rude but meaningful awakening to recognise a broader perspective. With each passing day, I am learning to be OK with being a schmuck. It is oddly freeing to acknowledge it, and I find that this basic truth about myself helps me to see other people more clearly.

Taking responsibility is another good place from which to start. It is a critical action if we hope to move in the direction of being egoless. Unpacking exactly what taking responsibility means has become a continual source of discovery for me. I try to take responsibility for my health, my energy and my ability to focus and be present. This extends also to my feelings, my fears and the impact I may be having simply by being present and what my presence may mean to the person I am facing. I try to be aware of and take responsibility for my power in the encounter that takes place with other people in my work. There is an inherent power imbalance in what we do and denying that is naïve and disrespects the people we work with. There are also a number of other power imbalances we must each face that are present in our work with other people, such as race and gender. It is also naïve to think these issues do not play a role in how we hear other people and how they experience us and their ability to open their worlds to us. I believe I must always make an effort to be aware and responsible to the people I work with. I care about taking responsibility for the things I do that might make the other person less human. Taking responsibility extends to how I use my knowledge or hide behind my knowledge, and for the way this expert power can be held in such acts as diagnosis, theorising about the other person and applying techniques to them. There is also great responsibility in offering opinions that will affect another person's life. For me, this implies a necessary respect for the personhood of the individuals who come into my office and face me in my work. If individual lives are not respected and valued as real and meaningful and as precious as our own, then our method and science surely are dead; or worse, they are deadly.

Throughout this book I have raised, directly and indirectly, the importance of questioning everything. I see this as a hallmark of striving to be egoless in the work that we do. I believe that egoless practitioners are willing to question everything that might be a barrier to understanding other people: science, theory, systems and practices. They are especially willing to question themselves. If we hope to let go of the things that trap us and keep us from understanding others, we must question ourselves. Letting go starts with questioning and raising our awareness so we can take action. Questioning brings an awareness of our attachments to things that are not real, that keep us from what is real in other people. Hopefully a stance of questioning also brings an ongoing capacity to recognise our unique traps, our mind killers, in order to let them go.

One of the greatest challenges posed by our field is studying it without becoming attached to what we learn, without over-identifying with what we have studied. Much of the work of becoming egoless is not about what needs to be done but about what needs to be undone. The rest will follow. We don't have to be alone in asking questions and questioning ourselves. We can find colleagues and friends who will question us and question with us. They are precious. When we find them, we should hold on to them and seek out their counsel. Perhaps more important is to let the people we face in our work question us and that we take their questions to heart, reflect on them and learn from them.

We may also find ourselves working in systems with questioning built into them. This is an opportunity for growth and learning. I am fortunate to find myself in situations in legal settings, such as trials and arbitrations, where lawyers question me in front of strangers. They question my methods; they question my biases; they question my findings. And they question my conclusions. Of course, it is anxiety provoking, but I always learn something new about how to do this work better to more fully understand the people I encounter. I often learn more during a single, vigorous cross-examination than in many of the graduate courses I have taken.

Questioning ourselves implies trying to know ourselves. This is yet another potential path towards becoming egoless in our work, and perhaps it is the most challenging. My graduate training offered experiential coursework that taught us about ourselves in this work through direct experience. I am not in touch with the requirements of graduate training programmes these days, but most of the colleagues I encounter who are entering the field tell me they had no such coursework. In its absence, entering therapy or consultation for personal growth seems reasonable. Yet I am struck by how few people I have met working in this field who have actively engaged in their own therapy, whether to address personal distress or look for personal growth. I believe entering therapy for ourselves is essential if we are going to encounter people in the work we do. For me, there is a disconnect when we expect other people to be open to a process we have not been through ourselves. It also seems like a natural way to move towards feeling more comfortable in our own skin, knowing better who we are, so that we are more able to face what people bring to us and not get in the way of hearing it.

Openness to ourselves prepares us to be open to others, to be curious and even excited to see differences, to experience wonder. Greater openness to others can also grow from getting ourselves out of our cultural comfort zones. We are surrounded by our culture from the time we wake up until the time we go to bed, without thinking about how this reinforces one way of seeing the world and being in the world. One avenue for breaking free from our cultural routine is learning, reading and speaking another language. Languages open worlds and change us. They give us unexpected perspectives. New words, new sounds and new modes of expression activate us in ways that are different from our more familiar language. We can't help but feel different.

I find that getting to know another culture also helps me to reflect on my own perspective and how my thinking is shaped and funnelled by the culture I grew up in. I think it is good to push ourselves to be strangers in strange lands. I enjoy travelling to other countries for this reason, taking my time to wander in unfamiliar places that stretch how I see and experience the world around me. However, travelling to other countries can be expensive and not everyone can easily get away from their daily lives and work. If we recognise how insulated we can become in our own neighbourhoods, even exploring other neighbourhoods may be an inexpensive and invaluable opportunity for growth. Fortunately, the internet is also not expensive, for now. You can unplug your usual comfortable connections to your culture and plug into the news and entertainment of other cultures for free and with relative ease. These days I mostly watch Japanese television with English subtitles and I listen to Japanese pop music. Doing this keeps me from being too comfortable in the familiarity of my own world view, supported by much of what surrounds me in my daily life. While it is certainly not the same as going out your door and leaving your country, thanks to advances in technology it is much easier to leave the comfort of your own culture while remaining in the comfort of your home.

Nature is an ever-present opportunity to listen and open our eyes, and it is all around us. You may be lucky enough to have a garden to remind yourself of what nature has to say in all of its incredible variety throughout the year. But you don't need a garden; you can simply go out your door and look around you. This often is opportunity enough to wake up to the moment and what it might be telling us. If noticing what is around us is too challenging, we may turn to more obvious sources that are perhaps easier to focus on, such as art. Artists have already done the hard work for us and created opportunities for us to see what they have seen and hear what they have heard. They are undervalued conduits to other realities, and they stand in as emissaries of our inner selves. On the rear entrance of the St Louis Art Museum is a wonderful reminder: 'Art has truth in it. Take refuge there.' As human expression, art is an endless fountain to return to and drink it in. The presence of art in the world is essential, and it is a gift for clinicians who want to learn how to open themselves more in order to listen fully to the people we work with. For me, music may be the best training in opening us up to encounters with other people, because it is temporal. Its flow unfolds the way people unfold their realities when they face us. The internet also gives us ample access to this extraordinary world of temporal art. All we need to do is take a little time out to tune in and make it a habit.

While exploring any of these paths that may lead us to becoming egoless in our work, it is essential that we also find ways to take care of ourselves. Take care of yourself. Easier said than done, and I readily admit that I need to take my own advice more often. The work we do can be challenging and draining. We may find ourselves soaking up pain and distress. If we are not nurturing and tending to ourselves, we set ourselves up to burn out and shut down. When we don't take care of ourselves, it also becomes more challenging to be fully present to face the people we encounter in our work. Self-care is as individual as we are. For me, something as simple as having time with my husband and my dog heals me, nourishes me, recharges me and reconnects me with myself. I love gardening, cooking, listening to classical music and watching anime. Each of these things gives me something that brings me back to myself and makes me feel more alive. For you it might be hiking or training for a marathon or meditating or sailing or writing or going out to the movies or spending time with friends over coffee or dinner. There are things we can do even within the more defined and restricted world of our work. I do what I can to take a break and do nothing for about a half hour before beginning a long assessment interview. I enjoy the people around me at our clinic, colleagues and staff, and I seek them out, even to just briefly say hello. I schedule certain work when I know I am at my freshest, when my energy will most support my ability to engage and be present. I have an ongoing relationship with coffee. I have a regular appointment with myself to meditate at the end of the work day. I take a quick look to see what my friends are doing online and maybe have a quick chat. I also give myself permission in the middle of assessment or supervision or therapy to go pee when I need to. It can be that simple.

For me, asking questions is also a way of taking care of myself. I want to learn and know about so many things and still be a student whenever I can. Asking questions is how this book began. In the process, questions led to more questions, and I have tried to find my way through them in a way that brings me more clarity. And the questions continually come. As I find myself doing the delicate dance of offering my thoughts and opinions in response to my own questions, concerned about whether I am sounding too much like I am preaching, I inevitably come back to the importance of attitudes over techniques. I was raised client-centred after all, and it is a natural place for me to return. Attitudes are a tricky thing to teach, and there is no real way to manualise them. Yet I find they are the heart of what I do and they come together in a way that I would also describe as striving to be egoless in my work with other people. Much has been written and said about how attitudes towards our work with other people rest within us, but there is another perspective: our attitudes come from the people we face in our work. Watching an interview with György Sebők, a master of classical piano, I was struck by the similarity between my views about trying to understand other people and his views on trying to understand composers in his art as a pianist. I quote him at length because he captures so much of what I hope to communicate in this book:

> The attitude comes from the music. I don't put my attitude on it. That, that comes from Chopin's mind. Not mine. I mean, it goes through mine, but I'm just one station that way. And I use very often the word 'inspiration' in quotation marks. Chopin doesn't need inspiration. I'm inspired by him. But I don't have to inspire

him. He was inspired. He wrote it. He did it and my job is to understand him. But understanding is not an intellectual thing. That if I play that, I know that it is in A flat major: that doesn't help me at all. But to understand why he wrote, what he wrote, what he meant, what was in his mind before it went on paper; and if I can transcend these black and white keys, and I can transcend my own muscles (they move the keys), then maybe I can get close to Chopin's mind, or Beethoven's mind. I can never get there, because I am not a genius. But I can always take off one layer after the other. And I've taught this kind of understanding. (Blanchon, 2010)

My understanding is in the people I encounter in my work, not in my theories, methods or techniques. When I endeavour to be egoless in my work, I see the other person as my starting point for understanding, for attempting to have accurate empathy for their world and their experiences. Science, theory and language are merely guideposts along the way. If I focus on the guideposts, I will miss the journey. The real journey unfolds when I am willing to set myself aside and face the person sitting in front of me.

References

Blanchon E (dir) (2010). *György Sebök: music as a mother tongue*. Paris: altomedia. www.altomedia.com/html/dvd/sebokmusic.htm (accessed 4 June 2019).

Name index

Subject index

Also available at **www.pccs-books.co.uk**

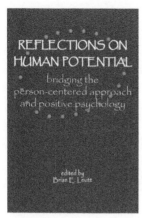

*Reflections on Human Potential:
bridging the person-centered approach
and positive psychology*
Brian E. Levitt

ISBN – 978 1 898059 96 7 (2008)

A basic trust in the individual is at the heart of the person-centred approach. This trust is reflected in the radical ethical stance of non-directivity and in the theoretical construct of the actualising tendency. In this companion volume to his well-received *Embracing Non-directivity*, Brian Levitt once again brings together an impressive international collection of person-centred writers. The actualising tendency serves here as a catalyst for a diverse and thought-provoking collection of essays, each reflecting on various aspects of human potential within the context of person-centred theory and practice. These essays, while shedding further light on the person-centred approach, also build bridges to the emerging discipline of positive psychology.

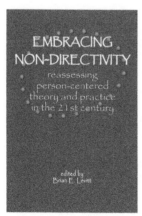

*Embracing Non-directivity:
reassessing person-centered theory and
practice in the 21st century*
Brian E. Levitt

ISBN – 978 1 898059 68 4 (2005)

Non-directivity is the distinguishing feature of the revolutionary, anti-authoritarian approach to psychotherapy and human relations developed by Carl Rogers. This book brings together an impressive international collection of person-centred writers, each exploring an important facet of non-directivity as it relates to person-centred theory and practice. Their contributions examine the history, theory, applications, and implications of the non-directive attitude. Non-directivity emerges in these pages as a way of being that remains vital and highly relevant to the practice of person-centred therapy, other person-centred applications, and psychotherapy in general.